Learning Along the Way

W0007019

Learning Along the Way sees Patrick Casement trace the development and application of his earlier key contributions to psychoanalytic technique. These include
his observations about internal supervision, trial identification with the patient,
and monitoring how the analytic space is either preserved or spoiled by the
analyst's contributions.

Throughout the book, Casement cautions against preconceptions that steer the
analytic process along familiar lines. He advocates a more radical approach that
is always open to being led by the process emerging between analyst and patient,
frequently leading to unexpected and fresh insights. This work makes a natural
pair with Casement's first, most celebrated book, *On Learning from the Patient*.
Here he builds upon all that was outlined before, challenging the reader further
and inspiring clinicians to re-think their established ways of working.

Learning Along the Way is an invaluable addition to every clinician's library
and an essential aid to practicing psychoanalysts, psychotherapists, counsellors
and anyone training in psychoanalysis.

Patrick Casement, previously a social worker, trained as a psychotherapist and
then as a psychoanalyst. He is the author of four well known *Learning From . . .*
books, of which this work is the culmination, bringing together in a single publi-
cation the richness of his 50 years of clinical experience.

Learning Along the Way

Further Reflections on Psychoanalysis and Psychotherapy

Patrick Casement

Routledge
Taylor & Francis Group

LONDON AND NEW YORK

First published 2019
by Routledge
2 Park Square, Milton Park, Abingdon, Oxon OX14 4RN

and by Routledge
711 Third Avenue, New York, NY 10017

Routledge is an imprint of the Taylor & Francis Group, an informa business

British Library Cataloguing-in-Publication Data
A catalogue record for this book is available from the British Library

Library of Congress Cataloging-in-Publication Data
Names: Casement, Patrick, author.
Title: Learning along the way : further reflections on psychoanalysis and
psychotherapy / Patrick Casement.
Description: Milton Park, Abingdon, Oxon ; New York, NY : Routledge,
2019. | Includes bibliographical references and index.
Identifiers: LCCN 2018025601 (print) | LCCN 2018031939 (ebook) |
ISBN 9780429793523 (Master) | ISBN 9780429793516 (ePub) |
ISBN 9780429793509 (Mobipocket/Kindle) | ISBN 9781138343535
(hbk : alk. paper) | ISBN 9781138343542 (pbk : alk. paper) | ISBN
9780429437267 (ebk)
Subjects: LCSH: Psychotherapy.Classification: LCC RC480 (ebook) |
LCC RC480 .C32 2019 (print) | DDC 616.89/14—dc23
LC record available at https://lccn.loc.gov/2018025601

ISBN: 978-1-138-34353-5 (hbk)
ISBN: 978-1-138-34354-2 (pbk)
ISBN: 978-0-429-43726-7 (ebk)

Typeset in Times New Roman
by Florence Production Ltd, Stoodleigh, Devon

Printed and bound in Great Britain by
TJ International Ltd, Padstow, Cornwall

To my supervisees with whom I have
learned so much

Contents

Foreword

Neville Symington

It is a pleasure to be writing a foreword to this book of my friend and colleague, Patrick Casement. It was in the year 1973 that I first met Patrick; that is nearly forty-five years ago. He and I were joint participants in an Infant Observation Seminar that took place in the consulting-room of Dr. Barbara Woodhead at No. 100 Harley Street, together with Paul O'Farrell and Daniel Ivan-Zadeh. I had just come into this psychotherapeutic world but it was soon clear to me that Patrick was already an *aficionado* in the business of clinical practice. He had already been working for some years as a clinical psychotherapist. So, he has been a clinical practitioner for fifty years, an amazing achievement.

A key issue for me is the answer to the question 'What is the underlying principle governing psycho-analysis and psycho-analytic therapy more generally?' I will give you first Freud's formulation:

> We ... turn to the ... question of what men themselves show by their behaviour to be the purpose and intention of their lives. What do they demand of life and wish to achieve in it? The answer to this can hardly be in doubt. They strive after happiness; they want to become happy and to remain so. The endeavour has two sides, a positive and negative aim. It aims, on the one hand, at an absence of pain and unpleasure, and, on the other, at the experiencing of strong feelings of pleasure.
>
> (Freud 1930: 76)

But this fundamental principle has been powerfully contradicted by the contemporary philosopher, John Macmurray in this statement:

> Freedom is, I am assured, the pearl of great price for which, if we are wise, we shall be prepared to sell all our possessions, to buy it. The ancient and widespread belief that the supreme good of human life is happiness – for all its persuasiveness – is false. Freedom has a higher value than happiness; and this is what we recognize when we honour those who have been ready to sacrifice happiness, and even life itself, for freedom's sake.
>
> (MacMurray 1949: 2)

It is clear to me that Patrick endorses the principle enunciated by Macmurray rather than the 'ancient belief' that the supreme good lies in happiness. The point is that freedom opens the person to an unlimited perspective on what needs to be endorsed and supported in a person's attitude and outlook. It also emphasizes the fact that this person's aim in life may be quite different from mine and quite different from what is often supposed to constitute life's purpose. It is clear to me that Patrick follows what Macmurray emphasizes. Consider these statements of Patrick:

> I keep in mind a question not often asked: 'Why do we interpret?' It might seem to be assumed that it is mainly through interpretation that we help to bring the unconscious of our patients within reach of their conscious minds, as Freud had been advocating. But we may often be interpreting for our own reasons, seeking to demonstrate our own competence rather than staying longer with a more honest sense of not knowing, until other understanding might later emerge.
>
> (p.2)

Patrick demonstrates here his openness to the aim and goal of the other, realizing that this may be quite different from his own attitude to life. He also realizes that what looks like an impartial assessment of the person he is treating may be at root a principle generated by narcissism. So Patrick continues:

> From there I move on to explore another clinical issue, which I think is also not often addressed, that of 'Imprisoned minds.' To what extent does our practice of psychoanalysis free the minds of our patients, or do some patients experience a pressure for them to give up their own minds in order to accept some apparently better ways of thinking?
>
> (p.2)

Patrick goes on to emphasize that it is a common error to attempt to squeeze this person's outlook into a system of thinking cherished by a particular professional outlook. He is referring here to the attempt to mould this person's mental frame into an ideology that is the preferred by the clinician. In a clinical account, written say by a devotee of Melanie Klein or of Winnicott or of Kohut, it is common to see that the quoted references at the end of the article are all of those who follow either Klein or Winnicott or Kohut. It is the moulding of the individual into the scheme of a generalized system that is very common to see in clinical work. Clearly, Patrick is not such a partisan devotee. He connects to the problem of this person, this person and no other. It is an amazing truth that of the seven billion people on Planet Earth, all usually have two eyes, two ears, a nose and a mouth and yet no two people, even identical twins, look exactly the same. It is also true that no two people have exactly the same problem to solve and no two people share exactly the same goal. I am preaching here but I have no need to do so when talking to Patrick. He knows in his heart that each person is different, and he respects and values the individual perspective of each person who comes into his consulting-room.

So we are privileged to be able here in this book to read the thinking and musings of a colleague who has been studying his fellow human beings for half a century. I recommend this book not only to colleagues within the framework of psycho-analysis and the social sciences more generally but to all people who are interested in understanding and developing their knowledge of this strange creature, *Homo sapiens*, who is so central an inhabitant of Planet Earth.

April 2018

References

Freud, S. (1930) *Civilization and its Discontents*. S.E. v. xxi. London: The Hogarth Press & Institute of Psycho-Analysis.

Macmurray, J. (1949) *Conditions of Freedom*. Toronto: The Ryerson Press.

Acknowledgements

This book covers fifty years of clinical practice. So who is there to whom I am not indebted for all that I describe here? In particular, I wish to thank my analyst, Dr Harold Stewart; my supervisors, Dr Adam Limentani and Dr John Klauber; and my consultant in the case of 'Mrs B,' Dr Paula Heimann.

This collection of previously published papers would not have been possible without the permissions readily granted by the journals concerned. For all of that, my publisher and I wish to express our thanks.

One person has been especially helpful with this book, initially in suggesting I might bring out this collection as a book and then in supporting and helping me with the MS: Dr Patricia Morris, psychoanalytical psychotherapist (UKCP). I also wish to express my thanks to Neville Symington for contributing a Foreword to this book and to Nelly Dimitranova for permission to use her image for the book cover.

I continue to be grateful to all my patients, from whom I always learned so much. In particular I wish to acknowledge and thank those patients and supervisees who have given permission for me to quote from my work with them.

I have eliminated identifying details from all those who are referred to. If anyone thinks they recognize a moment from their time with me (after many years), I trust that they will exercise their freedom not to identify themselves to anyone else so that their privacy can continue to be preserved.

As always, I have again had the generous support of my wife Margaret, without whom none of my books would have been possible.

Introduction

Stimulated by my unexpected reprieve from a near-fatal cancer (see 'My time with cancer', Chapter 18), I began to put together my thoughts about psycho-analytic practice in a brief synopsis, 'Ways of working' (Chapter 4).[1]

That recall of my clinical thinking re-kindled my enduring passion for this thing called psychoanalysis, especially after having ended my clinical practice with patients when I turned seventy.

So it did not take much prompting from a supervisee for me to realize that it might be worthwhile if I were to collate those of my writings that had been scattered between various journals and my own archive. Now that these are brought together I am hoping they may offer a useful presentation of my clinical thinking, formed as it has been over the past fifty years.

We have much to learn as we prepare for working in analysis, so it feels reassuring when we begin to recognize some of what we have been learning about when we begin seeing patients.

As we build up our clinical experience we may begin to develop a confidence, even a sense of sureness, as we proceed upon our way. But there are hazards in that sureness. We may begin to develop a sense of preconception, seeing what we expect to find. As a result, we can become caught in a partial blindness, whereby we may fail to see the unexpected, and whatever does not fit with what we may imagine we are finding.

Dr Klauber, my second supervisor, used to remind us that it takes at least ten years to become a psychoanalyst after training. It takes time to find our own way.

There is an irony in this because we are usually trained to accept the ways of working that we learn from others. And, of course, we need as much help as we can get as we start the daunting task of working with our patients. But whatever way we work at first, it is to be hoped that we may eventually find ways of working that have the greater authenticity in our being true to ourselves rather than borrowing too much from others.

Throughout this book I continue to explore different ways of working and different ways of listening, to help us to consider more than one way of thinking so that we might better understand what we are hearing from our patients.

Alongside this I raise some uncomfortable questions about the state of psychoanalytic training, in 'The emperor's clothes'.[2] Might some training analysts be hiding behind their assumed rightness in how they work? In particular, how do those responsible for training deal with times when things are going wrong? How often might it be that training problems come to be regarded as due to the pathology of a candidate, without attention being given to any contribution to such problems that might come from the 'emperors' responsible for the training?

Throughout, I keep in mind a question not often asked: 'Why do we interpret?' It might seem to be assumed that it is mainly through interpretation that we help to bring the unconscious of our patients within reach of their conscious minds, as Freud had been advocating. But we may often be interpreting for our own reasons, seeking to demonstrate our own competence rather than staying longer with a more honest sense of not knowing, until other understanding might later emerge.

From there I move on to explore another clinical issue, which I think is also not often addressed, that of 'Imprisoned minds'.[3] To what extent does our practice of psychoanalysis free the minds of our patients, or do some patients experience a pressure for them to give up their own minds in order to accept some apparently better ways of thinking?

In this book I am recommending that we consider the ways in which we may be intruding upon the analytic process, through what we are putting into the analytic space. In particular, I am practising with trial identification with the patient, in the session, and considering this as part of all internal supervision.[4] For, to be more truly in tune with each clinical moment, we need to be able to follow closely the interactions between ourselves and our patients; all of this being more immediate than anything we can take into our consulting rooms from supervision or from clinical seminars, or from our reading

Of course, my own learning from patients has been prominent in all I have done and written about. But here I include much that I have also been learning from my work with supervisees. And I want to make clear that in all of my practising with clinical moments, which I describe in my 'Further reflections',[5] I had been practising as much for myself (for other times) as for my supervisees. That is why I have dedicated this book to them.

I include three interviews[6] in which I found I was usefully drawn into describing things I might otherwise not have put in here.

As far as possible I have tried to limit overlap and repetition in the various papers that have been previously published, but I have retained some repetition in order to preserve the integrity of each original paper.

Rather inevitably, I return to the case of Mrs B, in the interview with Thérèse Gaynor (Chapter 16) as well as giving a résumé in Chapter 12, and more extensively in my response to Pizer (Chapter 13).

In 2006 Boesky said of this case:

> At present count, over twenty-five authors have given major attention to Casement's original report, and the publication of these discussions has

become something of *a cottage industry* (italics added) rivaling other famous cases in our literature.[7]

I may need to clarify to readers why I don't refer to the interactional and interpersonal writings that are, in many ways, parallel to what I describe here. As I said at the end of *Learning from life* (2006),

> I have deliberately not been reading these other theorists, while continuing my clinical work, as I have not wanted to be tempted to impose new dogma in the place of old.

That continued to be my practice throughout most of the time described in this book, at least from when I began to recognize the drive and direction of the *analytic process,* the essential value of *internal supervision*, and the sense of the *analytic space*. This I wished to preserve as a 'research space' within which it might become possible to explore further the potential of the analytic process, when this is sufficiently protected from the interference of preconception.

Here then, in this my final book, I present the core of my clinical work and writing.

Notes

1   Now published in the *International Journal of Psycho-Analysis*, 2017, Vol 98(6): 1813–1815.
2   Chapter 5.
3   Chapter 6.
4   Chapter 3.
5   Chapter 14.
6   Interviews with Kate Schechter (Chapter 15), Thérèse Gaynor (Chapter 16) and an interview questionnaire with Shelley Holland (Chapter 17).
7   Boesky, D. (2006) Psychoanalytic Controversies Contextualized. *Journal of the American Psychoanalytic Association*, 53(3): 835–863.

Chapter 1

On being in touch[1]

What I learned from my training about analytic technique was largely concerned with procedure. But what I learned most from my patients was to do with the analytic process: what helped and what didn't help. I give here examples that illustrate, in particular, the importance of being in touch with our patients at levels that mean most to them.

Introduction

One view of psychoanalysis puts an emphasis upon correct procedure and yet there is another that is more open to a process that stems from the patient. In my opinion, it is in this latter view that we find the clearest evidence of a patient's unconscious search for what is needed; and this is sometimes quite other than what the analyst might have expected or may be trying to offer.

Another puzzle, which I also think is worth considering, is the fact that we all believe in following the patient; and yet, in practice, I think we find ourselves taking up quite different positions in relation to the psychoanalytic process.

Of course, focusing upon procedure has its advantages, in that it offers the analyst a greater sense of knowing what to do, and the proper procedures to follow. It also makes it easier to teach psychoanalysis and to distinguish between this and other forms of therapy. And it is generally accepted that all analysts need to be firmly trained in the procedures of classical analysis. But if the procedure side of the dialectic is given too much priority it can overshadow other important aspects of the psychoanalytic process which I now want to illustrate and discuss.

My opinion is that *both* procedure and process are necessary aspects of any analysis, just as it is essential for a growing child to encounter the functions of fathering, which mothering alone cannot provide. I am also not convinced that these two positions are in any way mutually exclusive.

Childbirth as metaphor

To highlight the differences between procedure and process I would like to consider the different levels of function that we refer to when we speak of the process of birth, for example, and the medical procedures that sometimes go along with this.

The birth process has its own dynamic, its own sequence, direction and purpose. Sometimes, of course, the midwife or doctor in attendance has to intervene to deal with problems as they arise. But the supportive role is normally to assist in a process that has its own life and momentum.

Unfortunately, the medical procedures practised around birth are sometimes formalized, as if these were *always* needed, which we know can be to the detriment of the initial relationship between mother and baby.

Nevertheless, I think that there may be helpful parallels to be found between that view of procedure, which provides a framework that is available when process falters (as at a birth), and the ways in which we might regard the relationship between procedure and process in psychoanalysis.

In each setting there are times when it is essential that someone is there to act promptly and firmly, in ways that are informed by procedure. Without that a crisis can result which could be fatal. But, in an analysis, if stress is too often put on procedure it can mask the process that emanates from the unconscious of the patient, and the unconscious hope that is a part of that process.

Unconscious hope

I have come to think of the patient's search for what is needed as a process of *unconscious hope* (Casement 1990, Chapter 7; 1991, Chapter 17).

What is unconsciously looked for is an opportunity for previously unmet needs to be attended to. These include an unconscious search for understanding and for a more adequate containment of feelings that have been experienced as unmanageable. And the need for this is often indicated by the ways in which patients relate to elements of similarity found in the analytic relationship, which are then treated as if they were the same as elements of past experience. Here, of course, we have a rationale for transference.

I have been particularly impressed by the sense of a patient's unconscious search for what is needed from psychoanalysis. Even in pathology, when we begin to understand it in relation to a particular patient, we may find indications of what is needed for growth and for healing. And what is needed here is not only to be found in cognitive insight but in forms of relating. To this end, therefore, an analyst who does not resist the interactional pressures from the patient may be drawn into particular ways of relating which can eventually be seen in terms of this unconscious search.

Communication by impact

Because it touches upon the clinical material that I shall be presenting, I wish also to say something about what I have come to call 'communication by impact' (Casement 1985: 72–73; 1991: 64–65). I think of this as a generic term that covers all forms of unconscious communication that are contained within a patient's impact upon the analyst, in particular that of projective identification (Klein 1946) and unconscious role-responsiveness (Sandler 1976).[2]

If analysts do not inhibit their inner responses in the consulting room, patients can draw the analyst into an affective relationship which can do much to reflect, and to throw light upon, the patient's internal world and object relationships.[3] The analytic relationship may then become an interaction between the patient's internal world and that of the analyst, as an extension of it.

From another point of view, that of an infant in relation to its mother, Bion pointed out that, when a mother cannot bear to stay with the intensity of her infant's distress, the infant will be left in a state in which it 'is reduced to continued projective identification carried out with increasing force and frequency' (Bion 1967); and, I would add, with the increasing despair of ever finding someone able to bear being fully in touch with that distress.

I am not sure to what extent Bion then related his views to the realm of psychoanalytic technique but I have been persuaded by my clinical experience to allow patients to reach me emotionally, and as intensely as may be. I believe that this is essential, so that my understanding of a patient may include the communication of intense feelings, even to the point of my feeling them too.

It is one thing for the patient to have the analyst interpreting intense feelings as if these did not involve the analyst except as a focus for the transference; it is quite another for the patient to sense that his/her own most intense feelings are actually reaching the analyst, are having an effect on the analyst, and are being accepted as a necessary part of what needs to be communicated. And it is likely that some feelings can only be communicated in this direct way.[4]

The analyst can thus get drawn into being emotionally available for precisely those feelings that previously may not have been adequately received by a parent of the patient, or by any significant other.

Childhood trauma does not have to be thought of only as what has happened *to* a patient, which had been beyond the capacity of the immature ego to manage at the time. Trauma can also occur through *what happens within* the infant or child, when the feelings experienced are not sufficiently fielded by a parent figure being there to receive them. When there is no-one there to perform this basic parenting function, or when the person who had been there has rejected the impact of distress, that failure in parenting is also experienced as trauma.

So, in my opinion, the psychoanalytic process may need to involve the analyst in being *there* for what the patient is feeling; not only to interpret it but to experience this directly too. It requires both, the analyst experiencing the patient's distress, and eventually also being able to understand where this comes from, and why. However, too much interpretation too quickly, in the face of intense feelings, is often experienced by the patient as the analyst being unwilling, perhaps being unable, to bear the intensity of the patient's feelings. The analyst's interpreting may then be seen as defensive, and *it may be defensive*, deflecting (as others probably have) feelings with which the patient may still be having the greatest difficulty.

There can also be a problem with too little interpretation, when the patient's feelings are being directed at the analyst. Patients are often acutely aware of the fact of having had a significant impact upon the analyst. If the analyst acts as if this had not happened, this can have the serious effect of either invalidating a patient's perception, which will be confusing, or else the patient is likely to perceive the analyst as being defensive and perhaps needing to be protected in some way by the patient.

I therefore believe that trauma, in the face of overwhelming feelings from within, is the trauma of having to manage what cannot be managed alone. No wonder then that patients have often come to somatise intolerable psychic pain, or in some other way to split it off and/or to repress it. Unconscious hope is then expressed in a patient seeking renewed access to that psychic pain and turning to the analyst for help in processing this, seeking the help which had not been available before. But this will usually include the analyst having to be available for the patient's rage and/or despair towards the person(s) who had previously *failed* to be 'there' for it.

What I have been describing here goes far beyond a view of psychoanalysis as procedure. I also think that the therapeutic value of a patient *finding* what is needed in the analytic relationship may have been over-shadowed by a continuing influence of the medical model. That model presupposes that the analyst can be the provider of, or the master-mind within, the psychoanalytic process. And, it may be relevant to remember that doctors are usually trained not to be emotionally affected by their patients.

However, when the role of the analyst can be seen as more interactively responsive than is typical of any medical model, it may be easier to conceive of a patient unconsciously prompting the analyst towards becoming more nearly what the patient needs to find within the analytic relationship. And through this the patient may also begin to find the therapeutic experience most needed. The analyst may thus be drawn into this process in ways that belong to the unconscious search of the patient, and (once again) this is by no means the same thing as the *corrective emotional experience* (Alexander 1946) which is deliberately provided by the analyst.

* * *

An extended example

I now wish to give some vignettes from my work with a patient who, in my opinion, had been engaged in a psychoanalytic process from his first meeting with me, even though it took him several years before he found his own way to five times per week analysis. Incidentally, though I say that the patient had been engaged in a psychoanalytic process, it would be more accurate to say that *he had engaged me* in this process.

Background

This patient (I shall call him Mr A) was quite young when he came to me. For much of his first three and a half years he was virtually blind with undiagnosed myopia; he was unable to focus much beyond the distance of about one centimetre. His development was therefore far from normal, but his parents seem to have interpreted his strange behaviour to mean that he was mentally subnormal, or perhaps even brain damaged. Later on, they also criticized him for being a 'clinging' child because he would try to hold onto his mother's clothes. Inevitably, in his own world, he became completely disorientated when he was no longer in physical contact.

After his myopia had been recognized, when he was aged three and a half, Mr A was fitted with very thick glasses; he then began to find his way around the world that he had never seen before. But he had to do this in his own way. He had to touch what he now could see before he could recognize what it was.

Of course, there are interesting parallels between Mr A's experience of his first years and that of other blind children. But there is one major difference. Blind children are usually known to be blind much earlier than this child was. However, Mr A's parents appear to have continued to treat him as if he were sighted but in some *other* way not normal.

A major consequence for Mr A was that he had not only been deprived of any focussed view of the world around him, he was also deprived of anyone understanding his experience of near-blindness or the effects of this not being recognized. This lack of understanding turned out to be at least as great a deprivation for him as his lack of sight had been, and for a long time it left an almost unbridgeable gulf in his relationship to his mother.

When Mr A began school it soon emerged that he was unusually quick at mathematics. He believes that his early years of having to make sense of a world he could not see may have served to prepare him for abstract thinking, because when he came to mathematics it seemed as if it were a language he already knew.

Mr A's father began to be proud of his son, now that he was doing well at school. He no longer saw him as an idiot. However, in his adolescence, Mr A's normal rivalry with his father was met by rivalry *from* his father. It seems that the father had begun to feel threatened by his child's brilliance in a field of study in which he had always prided himself. The father then began to denigrate his son's quickness in understanding mathematics, saying that he was 'being superficial.' The relationship between father and son then began to deteriorate, leaving Mr A (at that time) with no good relationship with either parent.

The treatment

At his initial consultation Mr A was asking for help with a recurring anxiety about dying. In particular, he experienced this whenever he became seriously short of breath, as in running or other forms of sport.

When he said that he wanted to come for only one session a week, I showed some surprise and suggested that it might be helpful if he were to come more frequently. He then reluctantly agreed to come twice a week.

When Mr A came for his first analytic session I found him in an extremely anxious and distrustful state. He saw me as thinking that I knew best, apparently insisting upon him coming more often than once a week, disregarding his *own* sense of what he needed. And yet, I remarked, he had chosen to see an analyst rather than a therapist. He agreed but emphasized that he had thought (from reading my books) that I would be prepared to go at his pace, not mine!

After this confrontation I acknowledged that there was something important here that I had clearly not understood, and I agreed to see him at the frequency he had first asked for. Only later did he tell me that, since his first meeting with me, he had seriously wondered whether he could trust me as I had so immediately tried to impose on him my own ideas about frequency, regardless of what he had already said about it.

I soon discovered that I had slipped into being just like his parents in this respect, for they, too, had imposed their assumptions about him, and I had to take a lot of Mr A's anger about this before he could begin to experience me as someone actually prepared to take seriously *his* perceptions and *his* experience, of me and of his world.

It was only later that I learned of another key factor in this patient's history, which had been affecting his experience of me at the beginning of this analysis. He had previously had some experience of non-analytic therapy, in which a therapist had devised to shut him in a room, with the alleged 'therapeutic aim' of confronting him with his claustrophobia, which was his other major symptom. On that occasion, Mr A had felt he was almost going out of his mind with anxiety, shut in a room on his own. He subsequently told me that he had been similarly afraid of being tied into a frequency of sessions with me that was not of his own choosing.

In the second year of Mr A's therapy his wife gave birth to their first child and he was present at the birth. He had been greatly moved by that experience, in particular by the gradual way in which this baby had shifted from receiving oxygen through the umbilical cord, then to natural breathing. The doctors had allowed the mother to hold her baby straight away, without cutting the cord, and Mr A had been fascinated by the pulsating cord, watching the pulse gradually subside as normal breathing began to be established. His comment was: 'The doctors did not have to *force* this process by interfering.' From the emphasis in his voice, I felt that I was being reminded of his first session with me and his comments about the matter of frequency, but I did not comment.

What then emerged was the fact that Mr A had learned from his mother that, at his own birth, he had been born with the cord around his neck. The cord had been cut (which may well have saved his life) but he gathers that he had also been treated to the usual slapping of his back to make him cry, in order to establish breathing. Some of that medical procedure, perhaps all of it, had been necessary.

But it did not have to follow that I had to behave in any similar way. I now felt that he was indicating how he had experienced me as trying to hurry him into my idea of psychoanalysis.

I therefore said:

> I think you are telling me how important it is for you that I should let you find your own way into analysis rather than trying to impose on you my own ideas about this, as with the frequency of sessions.

Mr A nodded his head and I could see that he was silently crying. [Incidentally, I sit a bit to one side of the couch, as well as being behind it, so that I can see some part of a patient's face. I find this very important because so much is communicated in a patient's expression.]

Around this time I heard again of Mr A's breathlessness, and his fear of dying. When I made a link between this and what I had been hearing about his own birth, compared to that of his son, he again became very moved. I had said to him that I wondered whether there might be some deep body-memory of his experience of being short of oxygen, with the cord around his neck, and again when the cord was cut. He felt almost sure that this must be so. Why else, he asked, should he feel so relieved when I shared that thought with him?

After this session Mr A noticed that he was less often having the experience of fighting for breath after he had been running. So, something was beginning to change. It was as if his desperate need had not only been for oxygen but also for an understanding of his own very early experience of that urgent need, associated with near death. Shortly after this Mr A asked to come more frequently, first twice and then three times a week.

*   *   *

I now wish to describe part of a session that took place some months later. For some time, Mr A had again been telling me about his rivalrous relationship with his father and I was beginning to think that I should be interpreting his castration anxiety, but I had not yet done so. Then he brought a dream in which there had been a dog threatening to attack him in the back. I therefore tried to interpret this in terms of the current theme, suggesting that he seemed to be experiencing me in the transference as the Oedipal father who might attack him from behind. However, this meant nothing to Mr A. In fact, he was really scornful of this, saying that I seemed to be trying to force some theory onto him just because I thought that it fitted.

It was, once again, clear that I was being prompted to re-think. I also felt that I was being reminded of Mr A's experience of his parents who had for so long seen him only in terms of their own preconceptions, thus profoundly misunderstanding him. I therefore commented that he seemed to be experiencing me as the parents who had been so drastically missing the point about his behaviour when he could not see. He replied that he wasn't sure that it was that. Then, for no reason that I could explain to myself, I had an image of a doctor slapping a baby on the back to make it breathe. This changed the course of my thinking.[5]

I then said:

> Even though it seems like a sudden change of focus, it occurs to me now that the dog in your dream might represent the doctor who had seemed to attack you in the back to make you breathe. I think you have been experiencing me as that doctor, slapping you with my ideas of how theory might apply to you.

Mr A fell into a prolonged silence, again with tears spilling down his face for the rest of the session.

I had been surprised at myself for making such a leap back from adolescence (where the patient had seemed to be) to something so very early. However, in the following session Mr A gave me his own view of this.

Before that moment in the previous session he had experienced me as pushing on with his Oedipal relationship to his father, as if that made me feel on more familiar ground analytically. I *had* therefore become like the doctor at his birth, who (after the cord had been cut) had been hitting him in the back. Consequently, he had experienced my shift of focus as a sudden relief, and it had prompted him to think that I could (after all) allow him to go at his own pace, when I was more prepared to follow his cues. Perhaps I would, after all, allow him to make his own transition from one mode of breathing to another, like his baby son.

Soon after this he again asked to increase his sessions, this time to four times per week, which I agreed to as soon as a suitable vacancy became available.

* * *

I would now like to give a brief impression of a later phase in my work with this patient.

There had been some occasions when I could not understand, even approximately, what Mr A was trying to communicate to me. At such times he was often being elliptical in what he was saying, so that it seemed not to come into focus for me. Eventually, I realized that it was as if I were being drawn into something of his own experience of not being able to see, which I began to understand in terms of projective identification, his difficult experience being evoked in me. Therefore, when this was happening again in a session I said to him:

> There are times, like to-day, when I have had to realize that I cannot understand what you are saying. I am not sure whether this is because I am really missing something, or whether it may be that you are somehow communicating to me some of *your experience* of not being able to see clearly.

Mr A once again became deeply moved. For some time he had been experiencing me as the parents who were blind to the fact that he was almost blind. Now that I was beginning to see the limits to my own way of seeing he began to feel that I was getting nearer to his experience of blindness. New possibilities could then begin to open up when I could dare to move beyond the limitations of what I might be expecting to see in this analysis.[6]

Comment

As well as my picking up the projective identification of the patient's experience of not being able to see clearly, I think that I was also picking up some unconscious role responsiveness of the parents who were not seeing his situation for what it was. So long as I remained silent on this I was probably experienced by Mr A as the parents who were not admitting to themselves that their child could not see. But when I admitted that I had not been able to see what he had been trying to communicate to me, this changed. He could then experience me as *in touch* with him and, in this sense, different from his parents who had continued to deny that they might be misunderstanding him.

* * *

A while later, when Mr A was working over this session some more, I said:

I think I had to have the experience of not being able to join things up, or to get them into focus, because the sense you needed to communicate to me was that things could *not* be joined up.

Mr A agreed, and said:

I felt bad about anything that was easy to understand, because things could not be joined up easily for me. The paradox was that I *could* join things up in Mathematics.

* * *

Here, I wish to give a brief vignette from a later session when Mr A had once again begun to speak in his own strange way, and I shall quote him here *verbatim*. At one point in this session he said:

My words are not other people's words, and their words are not mine. They only sound the same. (Pause). A dog is not a dog. Why is a *cat* not a dog? (Long pause).

It is hardly surprising that I could not understand this! He then went on to describe how he had come to learn names for objects. For him, it had not been a process of naming objects (as for most children) but trying to locate objects to which he could attach the names he had already learned. He did not have any of the usual experience of a child saying: 'Mummy, what is that?' Instead his mother would say things like: 'Look, a cat' which of course he could not see.

I said:

> I think that you are telling me about the times when my interpretations do not match with your experience. I am still having to learn *your* language through a better understanding of your experience, and how different this has been for you from what I might otherwise have imagined.

The patient replied, with relief and excitement: 'You are beginning to understand.'

The patient then told me about what he described as a 'hidden' breakdown that he had when he was sixteen. He had come to realize that he had two languages; to other people they sounded the same but they were not the same for him. Both languages had the same words but the words meant completely different things for him. He had wanted to tell his parents that their language was not his, but he had been afraid that they would think that he was mad. His own language had 'full' words, but when he used his parents' language it seemed to him that he was only using 'empty' words. He said that he could never explain this to *anyone* as they would not have understood, particularly as he was ostensibly speaking the same language as his parents.

Mr A elaborated that the words he had learned, when he could not see, were the words that described his *experiences of discovery*. For instance, he could not know immediately whether a shape that moved was a cat or a dog. He had to find ways of working out which it was.

Similarly, whenever he took an object into his hands, it was through touch and smell that he would learn to identify it. (In all of this his experience had been very similar to that of a fully blind child.) But, when he was given glasses he had to name everything again, naming objects that were now visible. The names then given to objects were the same as he had used before, but the 'new' names had no sense of discovery about them. They merely attached names to objects, now that they could be seen, by-passing the whole process of having to work out what an object was.

So, when other people used names they were speaking of their own experience of identifying objects through seeing them. He found no way of communicating his quite different experience of having had to work things out for himself. But he could sense, from my responses to what he was telling me, that I was now beginning to understand the *considerable* difference for him between the inner language of discovery and the external language of naming. He became deeply moved by my being able to understand this.

Shortly after that Mr A had a dream.

In this dream he had gone to see a new house, with his wife and the two children that they then had. At first he was concerned that the house would not be suitable. There was no bedroom for the children near enough to their parents' bedroom, so they might call out in the night and not be heard. Then he found a room that he had not seen before, which was just right; it was next door to the parental room. The house now seemed to be exactly what they were looking for.

The dream continued:

Downstairs was an amazing room. It had a huge French window looking out onto a garden and the garden came right into the house.

When associating to the dream Mr A first spoke of his experience in the analysis, in which he felt that I had helped him to find a place for the child in himself, near enough to a parent-person who could hear his cries of distress. He was beginning to feel more secure now. He no longer felt so isolated.

Mr A then spoke about the garden room:

The garden formed a bridge between the inside and the outside. Your understanding of the two languages has provided a bridge.

I added: 'Yes, a bridge between your internal world, which includes the isolated world of your early years, and the world of others.' He agreed with enthusiasm.

Mr A subsequently referred to this time as one of the most important moments in the analysis. He had never before been able to communicate his sense of having two languages; one that he thought of as his inner language, and one of the external world that was the language of others.

*   *   *

Much of what followed after that was focussed around Mr A's experience that no-one had been in touch with what he had been going through during his early years. But the fact that I had begun to be in touch with his early world also led to difficulties, as it highlighted what had been missing for him in his childhood, that there really did seem to be nobody who understood the nature of the world that he lived in. He was deeply relieved that I could understand but he also found it extremely painful: what I have come to think of as *the pain of contrast*.[7]

Another outcome of this analysis, for me, has been a different emphasis on the nature of interpretation, at least in the part of my work with this patient that I have described.

For instance, when I tried to interpret something that he did not see for himself, Mr A often experienced this as if I were trying to shift him away from his own unfocussed world into a world where value was given to seeing things more clearly. But this was confusingly close to his experience of his parents who seemed to be so consistently denying the reality of his blurred world while they tried to get him to see things as they saw them.

The irony here had been that his parents, in trying to introduce him to their external world, were at the same time denying his experience of the world *as he knew it*.

For quite some time, therefore, it was necessary for me to be prepared to relax my preference for seeing things clearly so that I could be drawn by my patient into his blurred world, and to the quite different reality that he had experienced in that world.

It was in that unfocussed world that he had learned the names for objects that he could only dimly discern. And, in that world, a shape that moved in a certain way could at first be either a cat or a dog. Only gradually could he distinguish one from the other; and when he could do that it had been an important achievement for him. Therefore, his words 'cat' and 'dog' had been the names he had given to the whole process of discovery, and what he had come to think of as *full words*.

But the words 'cat' and 'dog' in the sighted world came to mean something very different for him. Other people used those words to name what they could see, but words used in that way were for him *empty words*; there was no sense of *discovery* about them.

The gains for this patient, in his analysis, have not just been those in which I'd been able to interpret what he could not understand on his own. What he seems to have valued far more was the extent to which I became able to learn the *language* of his pre-sighted world, and his discovery that he could communicate what he seemed never to have been able to communicate to anyone before.

Further comments

What I have been trying to highlight in this paper are some of the dynamics within psychoanalysis, through which the analyst can allow him/herself to be drawn into a process that emanates from the patient, and from the patient's unconscious search. In my experience, the analyst does not lose authority or effectiveness by allowing the patient more of a part in this process.

I think that we may sometimes miss what is most important if we think of the psychoanalytic process only in terms of procedure, as if it were an artefact of our technique. If we trust in the process, and in the unconscious, we are presented with unconscious cues that indicate when a patient is needing the analyst to be relating differently. And I wish to stress here that I am speaking of *need*, not of *wish*. But, I do know that some analysts have a view of the unconscious that leads them to feel that the *Ucs* cannot be trusted to indicate more of what is needed in the process of an analysis. I would like analysts to be able to re-think that view of the unconscious, in order to see more clearly the creative potential of the *Ucs* as an essential part of the process of an analysis.

At times the analyst will be drawn into being there for the patient in ways that are appropriate to regression, whereas at other times the patient has to find a sufficient firmness to allow for confrontation when that is needed. This ebb and flow of process goes well beyond what psychoanalytic procedure alone might lead us to expect. It may nevertheless be just as much a part of a truly psycho-analytic process. In the case that I have described, I felt that I was being prompted by the patient's unconscious search for the help he had not previously found. In particular, he needed help with the painful experiences of his confused and often confusing early childhood. But he needed much more from me than my sometimes being a better parent. He also needed me to be there for his feelings about his parents' failure to understand him, and their failure to be there for his distress. Therefore, when I failed to be sufficiently in touch with his experience (which, as part of the process, was bound to happen) I, too, came to be like his parents who had failed him. I could then be there for the feelings that belonged to those parents at such similar times of failure.

In being there for the patient's feelings about his parents, I could do something to help him work through the cumulative trauma (Khan 1973) of those first years of his life. And, in being drawn into something of his experience, even to the point of recognizing that I could not see clearly what he was trying to communicate to me, I was getting nearer to becoming the parents he did not have but needed to find. He had needed them to *become aware* of the fact that they were being blind to his being nearly blind, and blind to who he really was.

Only through my following the psychoanalytic process, in all its strangeness, was it possible for this patient to begin to find those experiences in my work with him, along with some understanding of them, that could become therapeutic.

Even though, by some definitions of psychoanalysis, this patient could be said not yet to have been 'in analysis,' except maybe since he began seeing me three or four times per week, I believe that there was a genuinely psychoanalytic pro-cess in operation from the beginning, and this may have been stimulated by the patient's unconscious hope that I might become someone willing to be drawn into this process. I would, therefore, have got in the way of this unfolding of the analysis even more than I did if I had imagined that I could have improved on the process by trying to run it along more familiar lines.

There are times, as here, when a psychoanalytic process is operating which can be followed and trusted. Sometimes it is possible for more to happen in an analysis when we allow ourselves to be led by this process than when we imagine that we have to direct it.

Notes

1   This was previously published as 'Psychoanalysis: procedure or process?' (1993) in *Psyche*, Vol 11, 1013–1026. Reprinted by permission of the journal. I also wish to acknowledge my gratitude to the patient described in this paper for his permission to quote from our work in his analysis.

2   I regard *projective identification* (Klein 1946) as indicating a state of mind that cannot be managed alone, this being 'got rid of' into another whilst also seeking help with it. By contrast, I regard *unconscious role responsiveness* (Sandler 1976) as resulting from pressures from the patient that can induce the analyst to embody an aspect of some other complained of person. These forms of communication, along with the effects of a patient's behaviour upon an analyst, I regard as being different forms of *communication by impact.*

3   For those not familiar with the analytic notion of 'objects' and 'object relationships,' these notions refer to the analytic observation that we all relate to others in terms of how we see them, this being represented as an 'object' in our minds as if that were reality. But the external reality may be quite different to that.

4   There are other analysts too who have described similar views of the analytic engagement of the analyst by the patient, for instance; Symington (1986), Bollas (1987, 1989), Stewart (1992), Rayner (1992).

5   Of course there could be no mental memory of that most early event, but Mr D had been told about his birth and he had often wondered about it.

6   I think there is a very important lesson here for us analysts in that, thinking that our training gives us special insight into our patients, we can become blind to what lies beyond the preconception that is based upon theory or upon other clinical experience.

7   I first wrote about this in *Further Learning from the Patient* (Casement 1990: 106–107, 1991: 288–289) where I describe the occasion when the *pain of contrast* first occurred to me as a necessary and useful concept.

Chapter 2

A missed opportunity[1]

I am including this vignette from a supervision as I think it may be of value to others. The main point of this example lies beyond any potential or actual criticism of those concerned. Rather, my aim is to point towards another way in which 'enactments' by an analyst, or candidate, can sometimes be better understood.

Many years ago, I heard a training analyst describe some supervisory work with a candidate when there'd been a problem in the transference at the time when a 'training case' analysis was failing. I felt that an opportunity for recovery of this analysis, then in jeopardy, had been missed. With a different framework for understanding the enactments taking place, I think that a different outcome might have become possible.

The framework I am thinking of is to be found in Winnicott's notion of *the analyst failing in ways determined by the patient's history*.[2] I think that this way of viewing enactments, in this particular analysis, might have helped the candidate to hold his patient through what occurred, as part of the analytic process.

The patient's background

The patient's mother had died when the patient was just over a year old, at which time he was moved to his paternal grandparents. There he was brought up by his grandmother who treated him *as if she were his mother,* and no mention was made of his actual mother.

When the patient was five, his father re-married and claimed his son back from the grandparents. The patient was then introduced to the step-mother *as if she were his biological mother*, some story being given to explain her 'absence' for so long, and the family was sworn to maintain total secrecy about the true facts of his real mother's death and her replacement by this step-mother, who was in fact the third 'mother' in his life.

After re-joining his father, and the new wife, the patient was treated very coldly by this pretend mother, and her coldness to him increased noticeably after she gave birth to her own children. He could not fail to see that he was being treated very differently from the way this mother was treating those other children. He just knew he had never had the same warmth or closeness with her that they were having. He felt a misfit in the family.

Then, in his late 'teens, the father deemed it appropriate to announce to his son that the woman, whom this boy had been persuaded to treat as his mother, was *not in fact his mother*; and he was told about his own mother's death.

In the analysis it had soon become evident to the patient that his analyst was a candidate. The candidate was then subjected to frequent abuse and contempt from this patient, who accused her of 'being a fraud', of being 'a counterfeit analyst, not being the real thing'.

This reliving of the patient's relationship with his counterfeit mother thus came to be powerfully present in the transference. We will not be surprised to hear that the candidate was having acute difficulties in containing her own feelings about this denigration of her, particularly as her own sense of competence as a candidate analyst was not well enough established for her to be able to take this disparaging treatment with any degree of equanimity.

One day the patient came to a session in extreme distress. He had just been to a family funeral and had only just made it to his session, as he thought just in time. In fact, the patient had arrived exactly *an hour late* for his session.

The candidate, having that next hour free, saw the patient immediately and without making any reference to the confusion about the time. The session proceeded, as if it were at the usual time, and neither the patient nor the candidate made any reference to this. The next sessions in the week also passed without the patient showing any awareness of having had that session at a different time, and the candidate made no reference to this either.

At her next supervision session, the supervisor pointed out to the candidate that she had made no mention of the mistake over the time. He put this omission alongside other similar omissions by the candidate, who then felt told off and determined to make good her error.

When she next saw this patient, the candidate drew his attention to the fact that he had come an hour late for one session in the previous week, and that the patient had made no reference to this then or in any of the sessions since.

The patient was at first confused and shocked, saying he had not been aware of this mistake until now. He then attacked the candidate, saying that there had been no need to keep him in ignorance about this. His 'analyst' had known that the session had not been a 'real-time session,' but a session that *pretended* to be at the usual time. She had deceived the patient and she clearly could not be trusted. The session had continued in this vein and had ended badly.

The patient never came back but wrote to the candidate saying he was terminating the analysis, adding that as a candidate she clearly lacked the competence to be his analyst and in addition she could not be trusted. The letter ended with the patient saying that *if he changed his mind* he would get back in touch. He never contacted the candidate again, and the candidate (as far as I could make out from the presentation) never wrote back to the patient, not even in reply to this last communication.

Discussion

The supervisor seemed to feel that this analysis was doomed anyway, and he defended his handling of that last supervision (before the analysis ended) in terms of the analysis as a whole.

The counterfeit session, pretending to be at the usual time, was seen as a traumatic repetition, to which the patient might well have a strong reaction. There did not seem to have been any specific attention given to the further repetition that would be involved in telling the patient the truth about that session. It seemed as if the candidate was left to walk into this further enactment, with the almost inevitable result that she then re-enacted the father's telling the truth about the pretend mother.

I felt that this situation contained the potential for real movement in the analysis, as well as the risk of its failure. To have held it through the traumatic repetitions, the candidate needed a framework that might have helped to make sense of what was then happening in this analysis and, maybe, could have helped to contain the situation.

I think that it would have been a help for the supervisor to have used Winnicott's notion of the patient's *use of the analyst's failures*,[3] to have then prepared the candidate to say something along the following lines to the patient:

> It sometimes happens that key details of past experience come to be repeated between an analyst and a patient. Now, by some strange interplay between your unconscious and mine we have reproduced between us two central aspects of your past experience. I believe this to be an essential part of the process of this analysis, and we will need to find a way to deal with whatever your feelings may be about this.

> When I saw you for your session after you had been to the family funeral I saw you straight away, as you were in such obvious distress, and it did not seem right just then to point out to you that you were an hour late for your session. But in seeing you when I did, without clarifying that it was not at your usual time, I became in effect just like your pretend mother. It was as if I was pretending the session was your usual real session. Now, in clarifying this to you, I am then inevitably in a position very similar to that of your father, when he was telling you the truth about your stepmother. It is therefore very important that we spend some time in thinking about this together, and in listening carefully to your feelings about this.

I would of course have preferred this to have been said in an actual session with the patient. But, when the patient had walked out, if I had still not managed to say any of this to the patient, I think that a case could have been made for trying to find a way of saying some of this, even in a letter. At least that would have been an attempt still to reach out to the patient, with the aim that he could begin to explore this further in the analysis. If I had been the supervisor here, I would have wanted to help this candidate formulate a letter somewhat along the lines I spell out above.

And now, one final comment on this interesting vignette.

We can see that the very thing about which the patient had the strongest feelings, around the pretence and the deception, and the father's eventual telling to him the truth about his mother, all these key issues were at the point of being focussed upon the candidate. They had come to be enacted by the candidate in ways that seem to have been uncannily determined by the history, for they are so exactly parallel.

There had then been a possibility that the central traumas in this patient's life could have been worked through in the transference, with the candidate representing, at different times, the pretend mother and the father who had been so clumsily telling him (belatedly) the truth. The candidate could then have been there for the very feelings that no-one else had been there for.

A period of strongly negative transference following this might, over time, have provided the patient with a possibility of working this through with his analyst, with someone (hopefully) prepared and able to stand the intensity of his anger and hate in relation to just those issues.

In the absence of Winnicott's view of this kind of interaction, the candidate lacked the framework that might have helped her to find a way through this. She thus did not remain available to the patient's most difficult feelings. However, with that different framework of understanding, she might have become able to work this through with her patient, in perhaps a very productive time in that analysis.

What a shame that opportunity was lost: a loss for both the candidate and for the patient. We can all gain something through trying to learn from missed opportunities such as this.

Notes

1   I much appreciate the permission to publish granted by the supervising analyst in this case.
2   Winnicott 1965: 258–259.
3   Winnicott 1965: Chapter 23.

Chapter 3

Towards autonomy
Some thoughts on psychoanalytic supervision[1]

I wish to make clear that, in this chapter and elsewhere throughout this book, I am trying to foster a process of internal supervision with those I supervise. To that end I explore some of the implications illustrated in the examples I give, trying to indicate opportunities to practice for another time. I believe that there is little to be gained from a supervisor simply being critical about things that are now in the past. Instead, it may be possible to explore how similar issues, as they arise in later clinical work, might be handled differently.

Paula Heimann used to point out to student psychoanalysts that it is useful to bear in mind, from the very beginning, that one of the aims of an analysis is for the patient to reach the point of not needing the analyst. In many ways the same is true of psychoanalytic supervision.[2] I have therefore chosen a title for this chapter which reflects that aim: the ultimate autonomy of the supervisee.

My examples are from the supervision of student psychotherapists but I believe that the principles I shall describe are also relevant to the supervision of analysts and analytical psychotherapists, qualified or not, and so are many of the issues illustrated.

I shall not attempt any over-all view of supervision or the different phases of this. But, within the ambit of my title, I plan to focus on a few concepts that I have found useful.

The supervisory triad

I wish to begin with some thoughts on the supportive function of formal supervision, as there are crucial dynamics which can operate in the supervisory triad of the supervisor, the student, and the patient. (See also Crick 1991, for a consumer's view of this triangle in supervision). These dynamics can be overlooked with consequences that are sometimes serious and unjust.

The role of supervisor needs to be that of supporting the student *as therapist to the patient*. This means believing in, and fostering, the potential in the student to become a competent therapist to the patient.

If the supervisor is not able to believe in that potential then there is already something wrong, either in the selection of the student or in the selection of this student's training patient or supervisor!

There are a number of ways in which the supervisory triad can break down. Too strong a model of how the analysis 'should' be done can be profoundly undermining of the student's own thinking. This can foster an exaggerated dependence on the supervisor so that a student can sometimes feel reduced to being a messenger between the patient and the supervisor, as if the supervisor were the patient's real analyst/therapist. There is also a problem when students feel that supervisory insights should not be allowed to go to waste, as this can lead to a tendency to use, inappropriately, too much of the supervision in an ensuing session. It is then likely that patients will sense that there is a different hand at the helm in sessions immediately following a student's supervision.[3]

When I hear too much of my own thinking turning up in a student's work with a patient, I know that I should not just question the student's lack of independence. I must also examine my own way of supervising.

Am I being too active in the supervision, too directive, or too dogmatic? Am I being too quickly critical of the student's way of interpreting? Am I leaving enough room for the student to develop his/her own thinking, in supervision and in the clinical work with the patient? In other words, I need to bear in mind what my own contribution might be to the difficulties being experienced by the student.

We can see a similar dynamic operating in a training analysis, as both the training analyst and supervisor have a part to play in the triad that supports, or fails to support, the student in clinical work with training cases. Therefore, when as training analyst I hear of things going wrong in a trainee's work with patients, I regard this as a prompt for me to review my own analytic work with that trainee. It is possible that some difficulties that a trainee is having with a patient may reflect difficulties not being dealt with sufficiently in the trainee's analysis with me.

It is always tempting to question someone else as supervisor or someone else as analyst when there is something amiss in a trainee's clinical work. I therefore think that we should always first examine our own possible contribution to a student's difficulty before settling into criticism of the student, or of someone else who 'ought' to be helping the student better.

It is also salutary to remember that a mother, when feeling insufficiently supported as mother to her baby, can experience her baby's crying as an attack upon her own capacity as a mother. At times of stress some mothers retaliate. Students can likewise feel threatened by a patient's failure to thrive, being dependent upon the patient for the training. If at the same time the student is feeling blamed by a supervisor for these difficulties, further inappropriate dynamics can ensue.

A student can have quite problematic feelings about a patient who is raising doubts in the training organization about the student's eventual qualification.

Even though students are careful not to retaliate knowingly, at least for the duration of the training, that reaction may surface later, however unconsciously. I have wondered about this when some patients are ejected from treatment so soon after a student's training has been completed. Another possible consequence of feeling that qualification is being threatened by a difficult patient is that a student may resort to pacifying the patient in ways that are aimed to prevent this training case from leaving at a time that would be inappropriate for the student. This can result in some patients being kept in treatment by means that are manipulative, even seductive, this being non-analytical and inappropriate to both treatment and psychoanalytic training. I feel that these issues are too rarely discussed.

I believe that it is essential that a supervisor, as far as possible, should convey a sense of shared responsibility for difficulties in the analysis of a training case. These difficulties often signal the need for more effective supervisory support, or more work in the training analysis, as much as they may indicate some deficiency in the student. When this dimension of the supervisory triad is overlooked a student can be left feeling burdened with a problem that can effectively jeopardize qualification. I would therefore like to see more evidence of supervisors and training analysts examining their own roles in relation to any training case that fails.

Internal supervision

There is always a risk that an inexperienced supervisee may invest too much in the authority and assumed wisdom of the supervisor. This can inhibit the autonomous working of a student at the time when it most matters, when the student is with a patient. I have described elsewhere (Casement 1985, Chapter 2; 1991, Chapter 2) the course of development from external supervisor to internalized supervisor, and the development of a student's own internal supervision as separate from that. It is with this last that I am primarily concerned in this paper.

It is not unusual to hear a student in supervision saying: 'At this point in the session I began asking myself what you might have said here.' I therefore regard the concept of an internal supervisor as representing the student's own thinking as distinct from that of the internalized supervisor. Both are important, what the actual supervisor might say and what the student is thinking in the session. I therefore try to foster a supervisee's sense of this inner dialogue, so that the thinking represented by the internalized supervisor can be processed, taking into account the immediacy of the present session. I consider formal supervision to be a dialogue between the internal and external supervisors.

The functions of internal supervision evolve from a student's experience of his/her own analysis, from formal supervision, clinical seminars, and from following the clinical sequence of many sessions. It is therefore fundamental that students become able to process for themselves what is taking place with a patient, particularly when under pressure in a session, in order to become aware of different options and the implications of each interpretation, and sensing when to remain silent can then more readily become the skill it needs to be, rather than being too much a matter of intuition or impulse, or (sometimes) paralysis.

For the more immediate processing of internal supervision to become possible, students need to establish a mental 'island' within which to reflect upon a session at the time rather than later. Along with this, it is also valuable to develop a benign split between the participating ego and the observing ego in the therapist, similar to that recommended for the patient (Sterba 1934). This allows greater freedom for a therapist to be drawn into the dynamics of a session whilst still preserving, in the observing ego, sufficient detachment for monitoring the vicissitudes of a session. This double use of the ego, and the capacity to reflect upon what is happening, can also help towards making sense of a therapist's affective responses to the patient, and sometimes of being flooded by feelings in a session, without being incapacitated by what is being experienced.

Trial identification with the patient

Another technique, which I often focus upon in supervision, is that of encouraging a student to trial-identify with the patient in a session, most specifically to consider from the patient's point of view how the patient might experience what the therapist is saying, looking for ways in which the patient's experience of this might be different from what is being intended. This self-monitoring is essential because it is always more difficult to interpret transference meaningfully if the analyst is also affecting the patient through the way in which interpretations are given, their style and manner, and/or the timing of them.

A very simple example of a supervisor trial-identifying with the patient can be illustrated in relation to a student's attempts at finding a focus in the transference.

Example 1

A patient had just been saying: 'I feel that no-one understands . . .'

The student replied: 'Do you feel that *I* don't understand?'

As supervisor, I took a few minutes to go through this sequence with the student, saying something like the following:

> Let me be the patient for a moment. If I (as patient) have just said that I feel no-one understands, 'no-one' here could include you. I could therefore hear your question as if you have either not heard me properly or as not believing me. So this question 'Do you feel that *I* don't understand?' sounds as if you are expecting the answer 'No.' I could therefore hear this as indicating that you don't like to consider the possibility that I might think of you as not understanding. If I feel able to be directly angry with you I might then say something like: 'Don't think you are so clever that you understand every-thing.' Or, I might feel a need to placate you by agreeing with you.

The student then reported the patient's response:

> Of course I am not meaning to include you. I know that you do understand really. But my father often made me feel so distant from him that it was as if I would never be able to get across to him what I was feeling, even if I shouted. He was always so sure that he was in the right.

Comment

From a sequence like this it is possible to demonstrate to a supervisee that the patient's response to this question may well have been to hear it as the therapist being defensive. The patient attempts to reassure the student, and follows this with a displacement onto some other figure (here the father) of the sense that the student had not been hearing. It therefore does look as if the patient had been anxious that the student may have to be treated with caution, as the student seemed unwilling to be seen in a negative light, as not understanding. The echo of this problem, now spoken of in relation to the father, can be seen as an example of unconscious supervision (Langs 1978), as if the patient were saying: 'I don't know how to reach you. Will I have to shout before you will hear?'

What I am particularly wanting the student to learn from this is how easily a patient can be deflected from being allowed to develop a negative transference, thus keeping negative feelings split off from the analysis.

Example 2

A patient has been talking about a recent TV programme in which someone had been telling a psychiatrist that he possessed a dangerous knife and he was afraid that he might kill someone. The psychiatrist seemed not to have taken this seriously enough and this person in the programme had then gone out and actually killed someone.

Following this, the patient subjected the student to a persistent enquiry as to what he would say in Court if he (the patient) had really killed someone. The student proceeded to focus on the question of confidentiality, saying: 'I think you are anxious about whether it is really safe for you to be confiding in me or might I disclose to others some of what you tell me?'

As supervisor, I felt that this was a misleading focus. I therefore made the following comments:

> I feel that you are staying with the question of confidentiality, in this hypo-thetical future, which may be easier to think about than the issue of potential violence referred to in the opening statements of this session.

> We have been hearing of someone whose thoughts of violence have not been taken seriously enough, phantasy[4] leading to action. If you listen to yourself

from the position of the patient here, you might notice that he could be wondering if his thoughts of violence have been taken seriously They need to be, as the patient is pointing out.

If they are not, the sequence might move into this hypothetical future with some actual act of violence. The matter of confidentiality is clearly secondary to that of the patient's violent feelings and phantasies.

Comment

Again, we can see a therapist deflecting from the more difficult matter that is current in the session. Here it is that of the potential violence. The choice of focus could leave the patient feeling that his therapist may be afraid of this violence, too. No patient will feel securely contained when the therapist can be seen as backing off from what most needs to be addressed in the current session.

Example 3

A male patient had been expressing anxiety about showing his feelings to his female student therapist, particularly crying. He added: 'It is *cissy* for a man to cry, isn't it?' He goes on to say how he has always been very careful not to cry in front of anyone.

The student replied: 'You are afraid that I might reject you if you cry in front of me.'

I notice that the specific idea of rejection had not been introduced here by the patient but by the therapist. I therefore commented:

There are two things to draw attention to here; the rhetorical question, that is asked as if it needs no answer, and your actual response. How might you feel, as the patient here, in relation to these two points?

When I listen to you, from the patient's point of view I could hear your non-response to the rhetorical question as your agreeing that it *is* 'cissy' for a man to cry. I am sure that there is more work to be done in finding out how the patient has come to regard crying in this light, and he will need to discover that it does not have to be that everyone regards a man's crying as 'cissy.'

Also, where does the notion of your rejecting the patient come from? I do not hear this in the patient's communication. He could therefore misunderstand you to be suggesting that, if he were to cry you might then actually reject him. I think it is always important to listen for those ways in which a patient could mis-hear what you are meaning to say.

We can better avoid that if we monitor what we are saying from the patient's point of view, not jumping ahead of the patient's actual communication.

Comment

I am using this example to remind the student to be careful to notice who introduces what into a session, and that a patient can regard something that is brought in by the therapist as perhaps revealing some unconscious truth about the therapist. This 'reading' of the therapist by the patient can sometimes lead to a patient beginning to negotiate with the therapist now seen in this way, a sequence that is not uncommon. It can become confusing if too much of the patient's reactions to the therapist are then treated as if they were only a matter of transference, unconnected to some recent reality in the therapy.

Example 4

A patient had been at a school where teachers used to speak of masturbation as 'self-abuse', and he now uses this term as his own way of speaking of it. The therapist reports a session in which she, too, had been using the patient's own words for masturbation.

I commented:

> When I listen to you speaking here of 'self-abuse' I am hearing two things that you may not be considering from the patient's point of view. First, I hear you being euphemistic, which suggests that you too may be feeling embarrassed by this. The patient is using euphemism here as his way of speaking of masturbation, but it will not help him to feel any more able to talk about it if he feels that you too find this difficult.

> I am also hearing you as if you, too, regard masturbation as a bad thing, literally as 'self-abuse'. The point I want to stress is that it is fundamental for the patient to find that there can be another view of this. It might therefore help to open up the analytic space, in which other views can be considered, if you were to be more direct in your own language, or if you are careful to indicate that you are not regarding masturbation in the same way as the patient. You could then refer to what he has been saying by referring to masturbation as 'what you have come to think of as self-abuse'. That could open up some analysis of how the patient has been affected by the attitudes of others in relation to this.

Comment

I am trying to illustrate here that there always needs to be a sufficient difference between how things are viewed by a therapist/analyst and how they have been viewed before in a patient's life. It is this difference that establishes the analytic space within which to think about things differently. If a therapist appears to share a patient's pathological view on some matter it is likely to seem confusing if the therapist then questions the patient's view on this.

Example 5[5]

The day before the session being reported, a male patient had been kept waiting by his student therapist. The student had not been immediately available when the patient had rung the doorbell even though he had arrived on time for the session.

The following day, the patient was speaking about someone at work who had been insisting on his keeping an appointment by being there 'sharp on time'.

The student naturally linked this to the previous day by saying: 'I think you are referring to yesterday when I did not open the door to you at two o'clock sharp.' Once again, I felt that there was something worth noticing in the student using the patient's own words back to him. I therefore commented:

> I would like you to be the patient here, to reflect upon how it could feel when I speak to you in terms of being sharp on time. If I say, as you did there, I know that I did not open the door to you at *two o'clock sharp* I think that you might feel rebuked for making a fuss about just a few minutes. In the session this language is coming now from you even though it is quoting from the patient's own words, and it feels like pointing the finger of blame at the patient.

> Compare that with the quite different implications if I were to say to you, 'You are raising the question of punctuality which reminds me of yesterday when *I failed to be punctual* for your session.' I am unequivocally accepting that it is my responsibility to be punctual and I had failed in that, never mind the matter of how many minutes it may have been that I was late. I think that the patient could then feel more clearly entitled to his feelings about my lack of punctuality, rather than being made to feel that he should not be getting upset over just a few minutes.

It may not then be surprising to hear that the patient responded with the comment: 'Well, it was only a few minutes . . . It isn't that important really.' It sounds as if the patient felt that his own view of this failure by the therapist had been treated as not important. He then dismisses himself in this, perhaps identifying with the aggressor, the dismissive therapist.

Comment

I am wanting the student to learn here the value of abstracting the more essential theme from the detail. The question of punctuality does not so readily lead to a sense of quibbling over how long or short the delay had been.

I also want the student to recognize that there is a matter of importance being presented in the transference, but which gets deflected here. The patient is entitled to make a fuss over a failure of this sort, particularly when it is recalled that he had experienced his previous therapist as unreliable. Is this new therapist about to let him down too?

In this session at least, it looks as if that anxiety is being brushed to one side as not important. The patient is thus denied the freedom to explore that negative transference here, which is so crucial to his security in this second therapy.

Example 6

Another patient, a woman, had been in a previous attempt at therapy which had failed. One specific factor in that failure was said to have been the counsellor's frequent cancellation of sessions.

Now, in this second therapy, the student therapist has cancelled a session at short notice. The patient has reacted badly to this and, in the session following that cancellation, she has made multiple references to feeling insecure. She has been saying that she feels her boss wants her to leave; her husband has been rejecting to her; she was late for the session because the bus driver, at the bus station where she has to change buses, had just driven off without giving her time to get on the bus. The student had then said: 'I think that you may be telling me you are not feeling very secure in your therapy with me.'

I commented:

> I think that your patient has been telling you very clearly that she is not feeling secure with you. We have heard of someone who may be wanting the patient to leave, someone who is felt to be rejecting of her and someone who did not want her to be on the bus, so that she was not allowed to continue her journey. This patient has already had to change therapists once. The idea that this second therapy could also be in trouble might well make her extremely anxious. She might feel in crisis about her therapy with you. She therefore needs to know that you are really in touch with what it could be meaning to her. It might even mean having to change again to another therapist.

> When I trial-identify with the patient here, your use of 'maybe' suggests to me that you are not really registering what a crisis this could be for the patient. Also, 'not feeling very secure' sounds as if you are again minimizing the insecurity the patient could be feeling. If you had listened to what you had in mind to say here, from the patient's point of view, you could have picked up these points for yourself

Comment

I make a lot of this small detail as a teaching point. There will certainly be other occasions when this therapist will need to be more firm than tentative, so it is worth learning about this now. A patient who is in crisis needs to have a clear sense of the analyst/therapist being genuinely in touch with this fact; feeling some of the impact of that crisis as well. It is not then enough to be commenting, as it were, from afar. But, the opposite problem exists too, that of the therapist appearing too sure.

Example 7

A patient has been describing a row with his wife after which she had walked out. The male student therapist said: 'You must have felt very rejected.'

The patient replied: 'I suppose so' and continued to talk about feeling that his wife had just not understood what the row had been about.

I commented:

> I am concerned about two things here. First, you say that the patient 'must have' felt rejected. Why must he have felt that? I think that you may have put yourself too literally into the patient's shoes here.

> When we try to trial-identify with the patient we need always to bear in mind that we are not literally putting *ourselves* into the patient's shoes. That is almost bound to be misleading as we are then likely to note what we might have felt in that situation rather than what the patient may have felt. So, in trial-identifying, we need to use all that we know about the patient in trying to explore what the patient might feel in that situation.

> If we bear in mind what else we know about this patient, we may remember that he has been playing with the idea of provoking his wife to leave. He also likes to put his wife in the wrong. So, he may well have felt all sorts of other things here than just feeling rejected. For instance, he might have felt triumph.

As we actually do not know what this patient felt we might be able to help him to reflect upon his own feelings here. It would have been enough to say: 'It is not clear to me what you felt about her leaving.' The patient could then begin to clarify this, if he wishes. And, in this particular session, I hear the patient replying that he felt not understood, *by someone*. That could be some unconscious supervision by the patient. He may have felt not understood by the therapist.

Comment

I would like to note several points about my response here. I am, as so often, speaking about technique. But I also find myself using the plural here, 'we'. I have sometimes thought of this as the plural of supervision.

I try not to stay too much with 'I' and 'you,' as if I am telling the supervisee what he/she might do. I think that can all too easily be experienced as undermining, even persecutory. I am therefore putting myself alongside the supervisee, trying to consider different options, speaking of what 'we' might notice and what 'we' might say.

I am also illustrating here the value of using a stance of not-knowing, as a way of encouraging the patient to reflect, rather than too often seeing interpretation as making statements about the patient's unconscious. We are frequently in a position where we cannot be that certain, so it is necessary to develop ways of enabling the process of joint exploration with the patient. This also creates a less confrontational style of working, which for many patients is more appropriate. And it does not have to be just a matter of asking questions, which can be experienced as intrusive and controlling.

Example 8

A patient has been in therapy for two years, as a student training case. The patient is now talking of ending. At one point in a session the student reports having said: 'I think that you are taking flight into health because you are afraid of what else we need to face in your therapy. And, if you take flight from this, you will find that you can't get away from yourself and you will eventually regret ending prematurely.'

I commented:

> I am unhappy about this for a number of reasons. First, 'flight into health' is jargon. Could we not find some other way of addressing this so that we do not invite an intellectualization of the problem? Secondly, we do not know why this patient is wanting to leave. It could be that she is anxious about whether she will be less welcome as a low-fee patient when she has served her time as a training case. (She had discovered early in her treatment that her therapist was a student.) Thirdly, you build upon your untested hypothesis (that this is flight into health) before you have determined whether that is even a relevant point here. And then you can be heard as threatening the patient with internal consequences if she leaves.

Comment

I think that there are important object lessons to notice here. Some students do slip into intellectualizing the process, with the use of jargon as part of that. Also, I want the student to notice when there is an untested hypothesis already being built on, which can easily happen in a two-tier interpretation. And I want the student to recognize the need to explore what the various strands might be in this idea of leaving just now, as there are likely to be several elements in this, not just one. In addition, we must notice when an interpretation can be experienced as a threat, and not just as a cautionary warning. Patients can be very seriously disturbed by this kind of interpretation and the therapist's contribution to that disturbance is, I think, sometimes overlooked.

Concluding remarks

As well as illustrating some specific technical issues, I have been trying to give a more general sense of encouraging students to learn about technique for themselves, within the ongoing process of a session.

Another step in this, which I have not illustrated here, is when I encourage students to share their own thoughts of internal supervision as an integral part of their presentation of a session.

For all analysts and therapists, as well as students, there will always be more to learn about technique. In most sessions there are technical points to notice and different ways of dealing with them. Learning to *trial-identify with the patient* is therefore a necessary step in learning to recognize what the issues are, the different options and the implications of each for the patient. This can then become a natural part of the process of internal supervision, which in turn becomes the heir to formal supervision.

There will of course be much else that is necessary in any supervision of a student therapist/analyst, beyond what I have discussed here. But I hope to have shown some ways in which we can in particular foster the autonomy that students need to have begun to acquire before being qualified to work without supervision.

Notes

1   This was initially published in the *Journal of Clinical Psychoanalysis* 1993, 2(3): 389–403, and subsequently re-printed in M.H. Rock (ed.), *Psychodynamic supervision*, (New York): 263–282, and in *Learning from our mistakes* (Casement 2002, Chapter 4). Also (in translation) in *Psykisk Hälsa* 2: 114–126 (Swedish) and *Psicoterapia Psiclanalytica* Anno II, Numero 2, Luglio 1995, 12–26 (Italian). I am including this (again) here as it is so central to my theme on supervision.
2   The main exception to this statement is that it is always prudent for analysts after qualification to return for periods of supervision, or at least for occasional consultation, as a way of extending their skills.
3   It is likely that some patients in treatment with student therapists/analysts could say, if asked, which session in the week follows most immediately after the weekly supervision.
4   I am here using 'phantasy,' as introduced by Susan Isaacs (Isaacs 1948), to distinguish between *unconscious phantasy* and the more conscious 'day-dream' or reverie quality of *fantasy*.
5   This example has been previously published in *Learning from life* (Casement 2006, Chapter 8.)

Chapter 4

Ways of working

A synopsis of contributions to psychoanalytic technique[1]

Encouraged by Fairbairn's Synopsis (1963) of his theoretical position (Int. J. Psycho-Anal. 44: 224–225), I am similarly offering this summary of my main contributions to psychoanalytic technique.

Internal supervision: ways of self-monitoring our own part in the immediate process of a session.

Trial identification with the patient in the session: to take into account the patient's history and sensitivities. This can help us to re-consider what we are about to say, or to consider the subsequent impact of our contributions to a session.

The otherness of the other: We can only learn about another person from that person. We cannot meaningfully apply understanding on the basis of theory or of earlier experience. N.B. *Similarity is not the same as 'sameness'*. Similarity is often misleading, as the other will never match our assumptions, and we should always be wary of regarding any assumed 'universal truth' as applying to all individuals.

We need always to be aware of Karl Popper's caution, as in:

> If we are uncritical we shall always find what we want: we shall look for, and find, confirmations, and we shall look away from and not see whatever might be dangerous to our pet theories.

> (Popper 1957).

The value of *non-certainty* which helps to maintain an open mind at all times. N.B. In Sanskrit, 'certainty' = 'imprisonment' and 'non-certainty' = 'freedom.'

Preconception and *being too sure* can always dull our sensitivity to the individual patient and the 'moment of now'. It is always alien to genuine analysis.

Communication in behaviour: There is so much that is communicated through behaviour. Examples can be noted in all areas of life and in the consulting room.

Communication by impact: As though inducing in the other some state of mind that needs to be recognized and truly engaged with. Also, in drawing the analyst into becoming some version of the complained of relationship. And much else.

Unconscious hope: Difficult behaviour is frequently indicating a search for something necessary that has been missing, as for adequate boundaries and/or containment. Or seeking someone really able to engage with confrontation 'without collapse or retaliation' (see Winnicott, *Playing and Reality,* 1971). Or in seeking emotional holding that has been absent. Also seen in unconscious prompts by the patient.

Better experience cannot be genuinely provided (as in re-parenting) *it can only be found*: and it may only be found through the analyst surviving engagement with what had been most problematic in a patient's experience. (cf. Winnicott's paper, 'The Use of an Object', 1969). Often this is found beyond the patient having been able to use the analyst to represent the worst aspects of the patient's self or of their experience with others.

Sometimes *patients feel a need to protect the analyst* from whatever they imagine will be too much to bear: as in exposing the worst in themselves, keeping it as maybe *just talked about* rather than *more fully engaged with*, emotionally, in the analysis. Or the patient may feel a need to keep an assumed *'monster in the mind'* separate from the analysis, it being regarded as being too much for anyone really to engage with.

Using sun magic: as in assuming that this is what keeps the sun rising. *It always seems to work!* Likewise, a patient may come to assume that it is only because of the patient's protection of the analyst, by not bringing more of the assumed 'worst' in themselves, that the analyst continues to survive. As in 'sun magic' it can seem to work every time!

I see *trauma as that which cannot be borne alone*. I find this useful as it indicates what, at least, we can offer in being truly alongside the patient, to bear such trauma along with the patient.

I believe that, *in the consulting room, re-assurance never re-assures*. It only re-assures the person giving it. And it is likely to be experienced as the analyst sidestepping whatever is felt to be most likely to be unbearable to the analyst.

Forms of *unconscious criticism by the patient* (of the analyst): by *displacement*; by *contrast*; by *mirroring*; through *introjective reference* (e.g. in blaming self rather than the analyst or therapist).

N.B. *Transference by the analyst*: as in the analyst applying to a current patient what has been found useful elsewhere, thus failing to see the patient more truly as the individual he/she is. And the analyst may continue to relate to the patient falsely because of what is being attributed to the patient *by the analyst*. This is not the same as counter-transference.

Practising with clinical moments for another time: to consider how differently we could have responded, i.e. learning from our mistakes.

Listening with both hands: finding more than one way of understanding (e.g. on the one hand it could be this, but on the other hand it could be that). Then looking for what may be most appropriate as an interpretation.

Unfocussed listening: potentiating a wider sense of what may be being communicated.

Using the language of 'someone', which also potentiates listening: For example saying, I'm hearing about 'someone' who's being unreliable/ inconsistent/ defensive/ critical/ controlling, or whatever, which could as readily relate to the analyst as to the specific person being referred to. Also, being careful to avoid saying anything that sounds too much like 'you mean me'. It can be more meaningful when the patient arrives at a connection to the analyst rather than too often being shown this, or given it as in a direct interpretation.

Finding connections rather than *making connections*: When an analyst *makes connections* it can more readily foster intellectual understanding, but through a patient *finding connections* there can be a much more alive engagement with what is discovered.

Noting the *direction of an interpretation,* as from *present to past*, which often deflects from the present relationship with the analyst, and can be seen as the analyst being self-protecting. Compare this with connecting the *past to present* that can better enable further working with something difficult in the present, which may be a moment of history being re-lived, rather than 'going down memory lane' that is always likely to be seen as easier for the analyst.

The analytic space: This enables us to note who *is putting what into this space?* And why? When this comes from the analyst, what might it indicate about the analyst?

We also need to note *the quality* of our input and how this can contaminate the analytic space; it can be directive/ deflective/ controlling/ prescriptive/ critical/ shaming/ and much else, any of which can impact upon the analytic process and distort it.

Likewise we need to note that *questions can also contaminate the analytic space*, either by expecting an answer (which limits the exploratory space) or in deflecting from what is already in process; and may be prompting the patient to wonder why the analyst is asking *that* question, then, and so on.

The use of half-interpretations: leaving room for patients to make something of it in whatever way. (cf. Winnicott and the *Squiggle game*).

Two uses of the spatula: either to shove down throats (as designed for) or *to be discovered and played with,* as in Winnicott's child consultations. This notion could be seen as a useful metaphor for two quite different ways of working with a patient.

The supervisory triad: (cf. Winnicott's nursing triad for a mother and her baby), the supervisor holding the supervisee who holds the patient. Likewise, the supervisor needs to be careful not to take over the treatment of the case being supervised.

   I see the natural *language of supervision,* for me, to be in terms of 'we'; for example, 'What are we hearing here?' and 'How might we respond?' This helps to maintain the supervisor's position as alongside the supervisee rather than standing over, judging or controlling, and so on.

The place of theory: *using this as a climber uses a rope,* to catch him if he falls but not to climb up. This can enable a freedom to explore away from a specified route, rather than using it (rope/theory) as a directional guide.

The pain of contrast: The pain of experiencing something good that had been seriously missing before, particularly in childhood.

Imprisoned minds: Do we manage to free our patients' minds or might we sometimes be imprisoning them with our own ways of thinking or how we see things, and in our interpreting?

Why do we interpret? Sometimes it may be *for ourselves,* as in trying to demonstrate our assumed understanding or competence.

   A caution for training analysts that they should remain aware of the temptation to get into 'wild analysis' in committee as if analysing a candidate who is not present, or in any way able to participate in building the assumptions being formed in relation to him or her.

Finally: The notion of *learning from the patient* was inspired throughout and sustained by my becoming aware of how mothers learn from their own babies how to become the mother of that moment, as looked for by the baby at each different stage.

*   *   *

I have chosen not to give examples here. Anyone who listens to their own clinical work with these ideas in mind could find their own examples that illustrate what I am saying.

Note

1   Previously published in the *International Journal of Psychoanalysis* (2017: 6). Also in *The Bulletin of the British Psycho-Analytical Society*, October 2017.

Chapter 5

The emperor's clothes

Some serious problems in psychoanalytic training[1]

However excellent a psychoanalytic training may be, there will always be an issue with regard to the handling of problems arising in the course of training. It is then very important to see whether the usual ways of dealing with these problems are adequate, such that students[2] can feel they are being fairly treated. Also, can it be clearly seen that they have been fairly treated? A lot of this has to do with the ways in which students are regarded during their psychoanalytic training.

Much of the uneasiness about psychoanalytic training has stemmed from the power exercised by training analysts and training committees, and, as a consequence, students' fear of failing. Any misuse of this power is usually more from habit than from 'mal intent'.

I am addressing this paper to all levels in psychoanalytic societies; to my peer group of training analysts, that we should each attend to our own part in preserving the process of training and evaluation from the influences that can threaten to distort it; to qualified members, amongst whom there will be those who can recognize some of the problems I mention as having affected them during their training; and to students, that they might press for changes when they encounter the need for such change. I also hope that students and qualified members can be encouraged to see that, when they become training analysts, they can be alert to these problems to see that they do not continue.

A brief look at the literature on training problems

There has been a great deal written already about problems in training, and Mary Target has provided a most useful review of some 300 papers on training issues (Target 2001). Also, more specific to the issues in this paper, Eisold has noted:

> . . . there are repeated references in the literature on training to the problems of excessive orthodoxy, idealization and intimidation, at least in the lives of candidates.

> (Eisold 1994: 786)

In trying to deal with these problems in training, important recommendations for institutional changes have already been made, in particular by Kernberg (1986, 2000, 2001) and by Garza-Guerrero, (2002, 2004). David Tuckett has also proposed important recommendations for the assessment of psychoanalytic competence which, amongst other things, could help to protect students from being evaluated on their character rather than their competence. He also refers to Kernberg, saying:

> Kernberg (2000) argues that vagueness about criteria for progression bolsters inappropriate power for training analysts and induces paranoia and passivity in candidates.
>
> (Tuckett 2005)

But, despite these moves towards improving psychoanalytic training, all these changes will take a long time. Such delay is not only because institutional change has to be thought through very carefully. There is also a perennial intransigence that comes into play in all psychoanalytic societies whenever the *status quo* is being challenged. Experience shows that there is an institutional resistance to change that is nearly always expressed in a long drawn out process of committee meetings, working parties, and often a series of society meetings or debates. Typically, all of this can take years to negotiate, often with the end result that little or no change actually happens.

An urgency for change

I began writing this paper because there was an urgency for change, and some changes could be made immediately without the delaying process of extensive debate and deliberation. I have therefore chosen to re-iterate some of the problems already mentioned by others, in order to focus more specifically on those things which I think each of us could begin to attend to now, without having to wait upon others to debate this. Of course, there must also be ongoing debate on these issues in order to bring about the more radical changes that will still be necessary.

I was further prompted to consider the subject of this paper as a result of hearing about problems in psychoanalytic training that sound very similar in a number of different countries. In fact, I am beginning to suspect that such problems are more common than is usually acknowledged.

For example, students' fear of failure is such that many of us know of students who have felt the need to edit their clinical accounts of sessions in order to leave out bits that a supervisor might disapprove of; or who have written up a modified account of some sessions before presenting to a supervisor or clinical seminar leader; to be interpreting as they are expected to. I also know of some student analysts, elsewhere, who had been taking unmodified accounts of their clinical work for private supervision, while presenting partly fictional accounts to their training supervisors in order to qualify. And how frequently do we hear of students, once qualified, who are later wanting to have some analysis 'for themselves', quite often with another analyst, because they have felt their own analysis to have been too much taken over or interfered with because of the training? I have also learned of some students having a period of 'supportive therapy' *alongside* their training analysis, to help them to cope with the trauma of the analysis – feeling unable to challenge the training analyst or to change to another.

Some of these examples are extreme and, I hope, exceptional. And we can of course put some of this down to student delinquency or dishonesty, as if this were simply a matter of their pathology, perhaps seeing this as a warning about the care that needs to be taken in the selection of students for psychoanalytic training. But is it only that? These observations may also highlight a problem in how students are expected to learn within a context in which a particular way of thinking, and of working, is often given priority over intellectual freedom and honesty. And, I believe, such constraints on learning are not generally encountered in a university setting, where free expression in debate and an open mind in learning are more usually encouraged.[3]

I have therefore come to agree with Kernberg, along with many others, that there are serious problems in any psychoanalytic training that may be inherent in psychoanalysis itself, and which should require of us in the profession a particular caution and concern. This has also been documented by Douglas Kirsner in his study of Psychoanalytic Institutes (Kirsner 2000).

In his *Introduction,* Kirsner writes:

> Once psychoanalytic institutes were established to take on the business of the administration and training of practitioners, inevitably certain dynamics, such as the corruptive influences of power, were set in motion.
>
> (Kirsner 2000: 10)

Even though he was focussing upon four particular American Psychoanalytic Institutes, where serious problems had erupted from which we can all usefully learn, no psychoanalytic Society is entirely free of the dynamics that he illustrates throughout his book.

Kernberg (1996) also shows that he had been shocked by the extent to which psychoanalytic students are subjected to pressures that inhibit autonomy and creativity. As a result, he was inspired to write, with deliberate irony, as if this inhibition of students might be a primary agenda of the training. Thus, with the imaginative style chosen for his paper 'Thirty methods to destroy the creativity of psychoanalytic students', he advocates:

> Refer all problems involving teachers and students, seminars and supervision, all conflicts between students and the faculty 'back to the couch'; keep in mind that transference acting out is a major complication of psychoanalytic training, and that there are always transference elements in all students'

dissatisfactions. A student's inordinate pressure towards challenging questions, imaginative thinking or developing alternative formulations usually has profound transference roots and should be resolved in the personal analytic situation. This means also that the faculty has to remain united, that teachers faced with challenges from individual students or from the student body at large have to stick together. A united faculty provides a firm and stable structure against which the transference regression of the student body can be diagnosed and referred back to their individual psychoanalytic experience [i.e. to their training analysis].

(Kernberg 1996a: 1038)

The power differential

It is inevitable that there will be a power differential between analyst and patient. How could it be otherwise, with the analyst claiming to have privileged knowledge of the unconscious of patients which, it is assumed, patients cannot know unaided? Also, patients usually expect the analyst to know better, else why would they come to consult an analyst? But there are many problems about being able to keep this differential within appropriate bounds. For without adequate checks on this, there is little to prevent analysts becoming convinced by their theories, with the result that their preconceptions can seem to be supported by their own reading of their patients' communications. The circle can thus close in upon itself, becoming a system of self-fulfilling prophecy; a closed system that can become immune to external challenge.

The power of the training analyst over students in analysis does not operate only in the consulting room; it can also infiltrate into other aspects of a psychoanalytic training.[4] For instance, the training analyst (except in non-reporting societies) has the power to give permission for a student to proceed in the training, and later to qualify. Equally, the training analyst has the power to hold up a student in the training, and ultimately to prevent qualification. Kernberg speaks of this as 'the most paranoiagenic instrument invented as part of psychoanalytic education.' (Kernberg 1996a: 1037). He has since gone on to say:

> I believe that the total separation of the personal analysis from the rest of the candidate's educational experience is absolutely essential, and that reporting should definitely be eliminated and considered as unethical behaviour.
>
> (Kernberg 2000: 114)

Supervisors, likewise, have this power. And so do seminar leaders, whether as teachers or as leaders of clinical seminars. It is no wonder that students often choose to 'keep their heads below the parapet' while they are still going through the psychoanalytic training. It is not without cause that this saying is such a common-place amongst student analysts. But what does it say about the training? It could, potentially, inhibit and impair students' learning and development, throughout their training, to be under a pressure to agree with accepted lines of thinking, and to risk being pathologized if they are too vigorous in challenging either what is being taught or the ways in which things are being done in the training.

Even when debate is to some extent encouraged, psychoanalytic students can still feel inhibited and remain concerned as to how they will be seen by their teachers. What kind of report may be written afterwards, especially when a student has dared to challenge a seminar leader? Might it go against the student when it comes to qualification? And the training is so costly, in time as well as in money, it could seem foolhardy to risk it all for the sake of one's own intellectual integrity.

I think it is mistaken to think that this problem is adequately dealt with just by having the system (as in some Societies) of students reporting on their teachers or seminar leaders, which they are encouraged to do anonymously as a group at the end of a course. It is also known that the students are individually assessed by their teachers. Even though there is now an openness about these reports, which students can ask to see, there is often a fear that what is not written in these reports will, in other ways, be conveyed behind their backs, either in conversation (however private) or in committee.

So, when there is significant disagreement with a teacher this is often not aired; at least not during the training. And when it does surface, after the training, there is often some bitterness added. In such ways much of the healthy challenge and debate, which is an essential part in deeply engaging with any subject, may be largely absent during an analytic training. And what a loss that is for *all* concerned – trainers and students alike.

How students are regarded by their trainers

Many students, despite being now more often referred to as candidates, feel infantilized while they are doing their psychoanalytic training. And it is strange that, whatever skills and expertise they may bring to their training, the already established skills of students are seldom acknowledged, as if these were irrelevant to the training or to the practice of analysis. (See also Kernberg 2000). But there is much important expertise that is brought in by students; other clinical experience, other frames of reference, a direct knowledge of other cultures, an awareness of group dynamics, academic qualifications and experience, administrative expertise, and much else. These important resources, represented within the student body, are seldom acknowledged. Instead, a much greater use could be made of them if the learning process in a psychoanalytic training were allowed to be more mutual.

Inner and outer reality

It seems to me as if some analysts have become habituated to the notion that almost everything can be regarded as a matter for interpretation, as if the only reality that counts is the internal reality of the patient. This view can seriously affect how a student is regarded when making a complaint about some aspect of the training.

Repeatedly, the power differential seems to win. For example, what happens when a student complains? If a student persists with a complaint, that persistence may not be recognized as a sign of health. Rather, a student may come to be pathologized because of it.

It is so easy for training analysts to interpret some *healthy* persistence by a student as 'being difficult', or as 'wishing to be treated as special'. And then, by a simple act of pseudo-interpretation, external problems, with which a student may be needing practical help, can be regarded as merely a symptom of some assumed pathology of the student. It would then require no further action, except maybe for the student's training analyst to attend to this complaint as if it were some 'acting out'. After all, a student who dares to challenge the training system can much more readily be got rid of than the system can be changed, even if it needs to be changed.

It is precisely because this power differential can so readily become abusive of students that training analysts need to be constantly alert to the possibility that they could, however unintentionally, misuse the power of their status. But how often do we hear training analysts being self-reflective with regard to something that seems to be going wrong with or for a student? The much more common impression is that training committees rarely if ever change their minds about students. Years ago, Pearl King pointed out:

> It has even been argued, when a decision of a committee was questioned as unfair, that because the committee's decision was unanimous, it must be fair and correct and therefore it cannot be challenged.
>
> (King 1989: 349)

When a training committee makes a serious mistake with regard to a student's training, the consequences for the student can be extensive. So, it is not surprising that these committees are usually reluctant to admit any injustice. If they were to admit this, how could they then square their conscience with the effects upon a student's training and subsequent professional life? How much easier, for all who sit on such a committee, to stick together around the notion that they have seen more deeply into the personality of the student than others seem to have.

Unfortunately, even after there has been careful debate about how to prevent major mistakes, with new measures being put in place to avoid them, there is a danger that these measures can then come to be regarded as now providing sufficient protection of the students' rights. But this confidence in the system can lead to a dangerous complacency. Thus, when some problem in the training is subsequently reported, it is still too easy to assume that the account of this is in some way biased or inaccurate; therefore not to be taken that seriously.

Wild analysis in committee

We also need to remember how easy it is for a group of analysts, like any other group, to get caught in a process whereby they may begin to interpret data to fit a given view. Alas, there is a particular risk of this when a committee has the unpleasant task of considering the clinical work and progress of a student, with the possibility of failing him or her. Such a decision is always onerous, and it is extremely difficult to take, so it is not surprising that any committee which has to consider this possibility will want to feel as sure as possible that they are making the right decision. And some students do need to be failed. But training analysts should be more than usually watchful of themselves during the process of coming to such a decision.

Of course, it is important that students are assessed on more than just their competence. Careful consideration has also to be given to the kind of person the student is. Unfortunately, with the change away from reports being received from the analyst (as recommended by Kernberg), however justified that change might seem, it does not deal with the issues to do with power in the training organization, and how this is exercised. If anything, power is instead handed to the training committees, most particularly the student progress committee, where it can be exercised with even less check on this than would be possible between a student and a training analyst, when the analysis is going well.

In the analytic setting the student is able to engage with the issues of readiness, and the possibility that some delay in the training might be deemed to be necessary. By contrast, in a student progress committee these issues can be handled without adequate checks and the student is usually not present. For instance, what happens when a student's 'tutor,' in the form of progress advisor, departs from being there to represent a student, shifting into the quite different role of recommending that the student should be held up in the training, or even be failed? Who then is there to represent that student and to monitor discussions about him/her, and the resulting decisions, for being both reasonable and fair? Is justice being done, and can it be seen to be done, behind the closed doors of such a committee?

Inevitably, when there is no reporting by a training analyst, there are problems for members of a training committee when they are trying to assess the character of a student, especially when they are looking for sureness about passing or failing a student. Training analysts in committee can then start speculating about a student's personality (almost as if the student were the committee's patient) in a way that could strengthen the case for passing or failing him/her. But the task of analysing a student should remain the responsibility of the training analyst, with only such other help as the training analyst receives from anyone he or she may consult. It is, after all, the analyst alone who has permission from a student (as patient) for doing that interpretive work. It is only within this privileged relationship that some analytic understanding of a student's mind and personality can be safely arrived at, with any real confidence as to its validity.

A key factor in all of this is that the 'patient' in question (here a student) should always be *present and able to participate* in any attempt at assessing his personality or character. Without that participation, any analysis, as in a committee, becomes 'wild analysis', and there is always a risk of assumptions being made that may then go unchecked. These can later come to be treated as if they were facts, which can lead to decisions being made upon a foundation that is much less firm than it should be.

Nevertheless, as training committees are run by analysts, they quite often get into a 'committee analysis' of a student, overlooking the fact that this process of speculation, in the name of psychoanalysis, is not a valid use of psychoanalytic understanding. Unfortunately, this happens so frequently in training committees that the members can take it as the norm, and this almost always goes unchallenged.

There is something here that can really amount to an abuse of power, but it is so common that it seems to have become a time-honoured practice. Yet it remains beyond the usual capability of a student to question this effectively, as any such challenge by a student could jeopardize their chances of qualifying. A potentially abusive practice, however unintentional that abuse may be, can become institutionalized with hardly a voice raised against it. But I have heard it said that *any interpretation given outside a consulting room is an act of aggression.*[5]

When things go wrong in the training

When there are complaints from students or from unsuccessful applicants, who feel that they have been unfairly treated in some way, how are we to regard these?

Of course, some complaints may indicate a pathological state, such as narcissistic injury for not having been accepted for training, or some immaturity in not being able to tolerate the frustration of not getting what was wanted. Indeed, sometimes there may be a wish to be treated as special, as in requests for some change in the training arrangements. However, committees can too easily think they see grounds for challenging student complaints, whereby they may simply be regarded as signs of pathology. One thing that seems to be least often considered is that a complaint by a student, or by a failed applicant, might occasionally be genuine and not necessarily be an indication of pathology.

Unfortunately, for a training committee to accept that a complaint about the training may be valid can sometimes mean being critical of a colleague. A training committee's judgement can then become even more difficult when it could imply that another colleague, particularly one on the same committee, has handled a training situation inappropriately.

Iatrogenic pressures within training

I believe we have to accept that there can be iatrogenic pressures within any psychoanalytic training. Let us therefore remember that it is not pathological to feel disturbed by mistreatment, but it can be pathological to accept it. So, what happens when students are being subjected to pressures that are adversely affecting their training, whether in an analysis, a supervision, a clinical seminar, or in dealings with a progress adviser? Most often, I think, credence is given to the trainers rather than to the student.

Some students actually become afraid of their supervisors, though they seldom speak of this to the supervisor in question. And (as indicated earlier) we sometimes hear of students who feel that they are having to comply with their supervisor's expectations as to how a case should be handled, even how and what to interpret. It then seems as if supervision were a matter of having their own ways of working dismantled by the supervisor, and the resulting void to be filled by an identification with that supervisor. The creativity in the student's own thinking and emerging ways of working can become stunted when supervision is dogmatic and/or controlling. It may be that a student is sometimes allowed to change to another supervisor, but not all students feel able to take this serious step as they remain concerned that it could be held against them in the training even though they are assured that it would not be.

It is also not surprising to find a student's clinical work being affected when, as does sometimes happen, a supervisor gets into questioning almost everything that the student is doing with the patient. Some students then come to be so anxious about how the supervisor is going to view their clinical work that they begin to feel watched in the session. They then begin to have an eye over their shoulder, looking to the supervisor and to how he or she might view things. Should the student say *this,* or say *that?* A frequent result of this anxious self-watching can be a student beginning to feel paralyzed when with the patient.

A similar anxiety may be evident when a student is about to present to a clinical seminar, becoming anxious about whether to interpret in his or her more usual way or whether to include interpretations that the clinical seminar leader might be expecting. The clinical work thus comes to be disturbed by these outside influences. Racker has referred to this as *indirect counter-transference* (Racker 1957), when a clinician is affected by something that is only indirectly to do with the patient. It is therefore unfair that a student's performance be critically assessed when these intrusive influences are not sufficiently being taken into account.

When we look at how things are going in the clinical work, we sometimes find that a student's work with a particular supervisor has begun to go to pieces. What might that indicate? Does it mean that this supervisor has been more successful than others in discovering a possible unsuitability of the student? Or might there be a chemistry in the supervision that is failing the student and which may be disabling his or her work with the patient?

I believe that the dynamic operating here is similar to what can be observed between a mother and her infant, when the infant fails to thrive. Winnicott reminded us that a mother needs to be *supported as mother to her baby,* if she is to develop the kind of confidence in her mothering that her baby needs to find.

But sometimes we see that the support available to her is the kind that is interfering. In particular, this so-called support is often coming from someone who presents as a 'better' mother. This is likely to undermine the real mother, especially if she is already lacking in confidence, with the result that she becomes *less* able—not more able—to take care of her baby. The baby then senses the mother's anxiety, responding adversely to this and thereby seeming to confirm the mother's sense of inadequacy.

We can also see that, when a supervisor's style has become undermining, a student's consequent compliance to the supervisor's demands may lead to a false-self development rather than to something more resilient and clinically useful. This is seldom acknowledged by other training analysts who may know that a particular supervisor can be like that.

When this kind of dynamic is operating in supervision, how are students to appear to develop unless they introject the supervisor's ways of working, to the point of becoming less themselves and more a copy of the supervisor? And when that happens, how are we then to read the supervisor's assessment of a student's work? The supervisor may applaud this development, but if the student becomes some kind of clone of the supervisor is that actually a sign of progress? Should we not be concerned at the lack of autonomous development in the student? Equally, when a student resists these pressures to comply is that to be seen as a sign of health or of failure?

In addition, if a student's training patient is failing to benefit from the analysis, because the student is being over-shadowed or undermined by a supervisor, whose failure is that?

When I made similar comments to these in my book *Learning from Our Mistakes* (Casement 2002), one reviewer picked up exactly this point.

> In case this be thought to be too extreme a view of things, a psycho-therapist colleague of mine went to a training psychoanalyst in London for supervision earlier this year and found that they were getting into difficulties and, after a while, the supervision broke down. Part of the reason for the difficulties became apparent when they discussed the purpose of the supervision; the psychoanalyst was clear that the supervisee had to put her own experience on one side, telling her that she could have her own thoughts about it later in her professional development but that, for the moment, 'you're here to learn how to do it my way'. It turned out that there had been a misunderstanding; the psychoanalyst thought that the super-visee was doing a first training, rather than seeking post-qualification professional development. Casement, one feels, would not see the distinction as relevant.
>
> (Hewison 2003)

Hewison is quite right in his assumption. However much a supervisor may wish to a show a supervisee how he or she works, I do not think that anyone in supervision should be obliged to abandon their own thinking in order to comply with a supervisor's expectations. But there are times when this does happen, especially when the supervisee is a student in training.

How do these problems arise?

Some hazards for the psychoanalyst upon qualifying

It can be quite a heady experience for an analyst to qualify and to become a member of a psychoanalytic Society, and through that to become a member of the IPA. There is a danger here for which some analysts seem not to have been adequately prepared. Unfortunately, when they qualify, they can begin to feel that they have 'arrived', with the attendant risk that they may begin to think of themselves now as *having been* analysed, as if they had been *fully* analysed. Some may even begin to develop a sense that their own unconscious has become entirely known to them, thus seeming to place them above most others, in particular 'above' their patients or 'above' students in training, who may then be treated accordingly. True, I don't actually hear colleagues ever saying they think of themselves like this; and yet I believe we all have to be careful not to behave in ways which could suggest that this may be how we have begun to think of ourselves, once we are qualified.

I know that what I am about to say should never happen. Too often we can see amongst our colleagues (who equally may see it in us) that this state of 'having been analysed' can allow for a quite free return of some of the very things that we had aimed to become aware of (even to eliminate in ourselves) during the course of our training analysis.

For instance, while we were still in analysis we had someone who was constantly there to point out to us when we were projecting, thereby disowning into others those faults that we wished not to own in ourselves. Our training analyst would not have allowed us to get away with this. And when we were being arrogant, or contemptuous of others, or whatever, we had our analyst ready to point these things out to us.

For some time after training we may succeed in remaining in a state of adequate mental health and balance, being aware of occasions when we might still be falling back into self-protective defences. Our own continuing analysis, now self-analysis, should keep us aware of those tendencies in ourselves. So, while that process of self-monitoring remains effective, all may be well. But what happens when this begins to lapse? Observing our colleagues, and I hope equally observing ourselves, we cannot fail to notice that some of these traits, which had been the object of much analytic work in the training analysis, seem to come back into play – at least in relation to colleagues, and maybe sometimes with students if not actually with patients.

For example, analysts can become extraordinarily dismissive of their colleagues, treating them even with contempt when there are differences of opinion over analytic matters. It is not so rare that we hear it said, or implied, of some colleague: 'He/she is not a *proper* analyst.' This usually means that the analyst in question does not work in the same way as the speaker, who of course assumes that he or she *is* a proper analyst.

It should be noted that this tendency for one group of analysts to adopt an arrogant position in relation to others is to be found in almost any psychoanalytic Society. (See Eisold 1994). It is certainly not a monopoly of the British Society, even though we do have our own predisposition towards this tendency on account of our having three groups under one roof. Within this nominally single Society (the British Society), fundamental differences may remain unresolved, frequently undermining the semblance of unity, which can result in this dismissive treatment of colleagues in relation to differences in orientation.

Much of this is a characteristic group phenomenon. As part of that group dynamic, some colleagues have pointed out to me that training decisions can sometimes be unconsciously motivated by a rivalry, or sense of triumph, over a student or applicant's analyst. I can certainly think of occasions when it has looked as if such a dynamic had been operating. And if it is *ever* true that a training decision could have been influenced by such factors, which in themselves may have little to do with the student or applicant in question, then we should be very concerned about the injustice that can result from such a contaminated decision.

The analyst's narcissism

In relation to the concerns I have raised, I think we should remain ever mindful of the analyst's narcissism. In fact, I believe that the narcissism of any analyst is that which most frequently persists beyond the training analysis, or most readily returns after it. Here I am not referring to healthy narcissism, as in normal self-esteem, but to narcissism that is pathological.

The pathological narcissism of an analyst can operate in all manner of ways, often unnoticed by the person concerned. I believe that any one of us can still get caught into problems of this kind. My purpose, therefore, is to encourage each of us to be owning more of what belongs to ourselves, that we might be more consistently aware of *our own part* in the difficulties that we have with those around us, including our analytic colleagues and students.

In particular, I am concerned about a widespread tendency for analysts, senior analysts perhaps more than most, to have difficulties in acknowledging when they themselves could be in the wrong. Instead, the wrongness of the other (particularly a student or a colleague) seems to be more readily assumed, not infrequently with some quasi-interpretation being used in support of that notion. Thus, projection may come into play again in the service of narcissism. Quite dire consequences can result from this.

The analyst's neutrality

> The analyst is responsible for ensuring that the thin line between use and abuse in the psychoanalytic situation is not transgressed. There is no substitute for disciplined counter-transference monitoring as a means of protecting that boundary.
>
> (Baker 2000: 131)

There is no doubt that the neutrality of the analyst, especially a training analyst, is a keystone in any analysis. As a general rule the analyst should never cross the analytic boundary between clinical work in the consulting room and the life of the patient outside it. And there are many analysts who claim, in relation to their own analytic work, that they never do cross that boundary, seeing such breaches only in the work of others. But, from reports in second analyses or from friends in analysis, one hears frequent examples of analysts, during an analysis, giving opinions about colleagues (for instance) or about much else, too, that is by no means neutral. And we sometimes hear of such double standards even amongst some who are ready to preach about what they see as the lack of neutrality in others.

Can any breach of neutrality ever be justified? Of course it depends upon its nature and most breaches cannot be justified. But if a student in analysis is being subjected to some abuse in the training, which no-one in the training seems to be aware of or which others choose to deny, what then? Doesn't the analyst have a 'duty of care' for a patient in treatment with him/her, especially when some mistreatment or serious injustice in the training is known to be in process? If no-one else is doing anything to stop this, is the analysis any better protected by the analyst also doing nothing? Or might it sometimes be better served, after careful consideration, by the analyst in some way questioning what is happening?

There are two completely different attitudes to analytic neutrality. It is clearly meant to protect the analysis, in order to preserve the analytic process. It can also become a fetish, being given monstrous status to the point of even threatening an analysis because of it.

One can see very clearly, in his published account of it, that Arthur Couch's analysis with Anna Freud was enabled by Anna's humane and sensible approach to these matters (Couch 1995). When there was a practical problem which was threatening to hold up his training, Anna Freud encouraged Arthur Couch to make a telephone call during a session, and I understand (from Couch himself) that *she then spoke directly in the session to whoever it was in order to help resolve an administrative problem in his training.* The analysis could then continue without being threatened by an uncalled-for hold-up, no doubt with this intervention and its implications also being carefully analysed. We can contrast that common-sense handling with similar training situations that come to be dealt with very differently.

For instance, I know of a training analyst who felt it necessary to speak to the secretary of a training committee, to help the committee to make a common-sense decision about a practical problem in a student's training. He asked the secretary to report to the committee that the problem, for which a practical solution was being requested, was 'a reality issue; not a matter of pathology.' The secretary, being familiar with the committee's view on this issue, replied: 'I think you may come to regret having made this telephone call.'

The same analyst later wrote a report on the student, whose training had by then been suspended, recommending that he be reinstated. This report had not been requested by the training committee even though, in the training rules, it was stipulated that there *should* be such a report available to the committee in those circumstances. As the analyst's report did not fit in with the committee's established view of this student it came to be regarded as being a breach of neutrality. The matter became even more complicated when the student's analysis then came to be regarded as having been contaminated by this intervention by the training analyst, with moves being initiated to have the student moved to another training analyst because of it. Ultimately the student stayed with his analyst and completed his training.

What was lacking here was any proper consideration of the analyst's judgement, that this matter was serious enough to warrant stepping outside the usual boundary of the analysis, and to have written about the student's situation and readiness to continue with the training. What was also lacking was common sense, without which the matter of neutrality was being treated as if it should have been adhered to as a fetish rather than as enabling the analysis.

On the matter of common sense, Couch also quotes Anna Freud on this. In the same paper he says:

> I recall telling her once that she had helped me see the value of common sense about analytic things. She said: 'The trouble with common sense is that it is so uncommon.'
>
> (Couch 1995: 161)

I think that this may be even more true to-day than in the days of Anna Freud.

What can we do about these problems?

From various discussions of this chapter I have received many helpful suggestions that are worth considering.

One important point, which we still need to think about, is related to the shift of power away from the training analyst to the student progress committee. Even though this might help to protect the student in the analysis, as advocated by Kernberg, we are still left with questions about how the power invested in the progress committee is then to be monitored and adequately kept in check.

Also, what about the role of the progress advisor? It needs to be seen that he cannot combine the role of 'tutor' with that of sometimes advocating a student's withdrawal from the training. When that happens a student is left with no-one to represent him/her on the committee. Many people have expressed concerns about training analysts having dual roles, that of a student's analyst and that of assessing his/her readiness to proceed with the training. But we are still faced with a similar dual role in relation to the progress advisor.

In whatever way a committee chooses to assess a student's personality and performance, it becomes increasingly clear that students should still be adequately represented on a committee when it is deciding their readiness to qualify, if not actually being present themselves. Also, there are overwhelming reasons for having a truly independent person present at such times as these, to function as an external examiner and to see that a training committee is acting properly and is not exercising its position of power unfairly or unadvisedly.

There are many more questions to which I am not suggesting answers here, and some of these will take time to debate. More immediately, however, there will always be questions that should be asked whenever there is conflict between a student and someone responsible for the training. At such times, I think that training analysts should always be asking themselves whether it is *necessarily* the student who is wrong, or might there be something else going wrong in the training that needs to be considered? Therefore, when a student gets into a tangle with an analyst, whether as analyst or as part of the training, does this have to mean that the student is the primary cause of whatever problem? Or, might it occasionally be something about the analyst, or some problem the analyst is having with this particular student or patient?

Further, it may be that it is not a matter of one being right and the other being wrong. There is often something to be concerned about on both sides when complaints are made about the training, even if a student is also seen as someone who can be difficult. And being difficult, in the sense of being prepared to stand up to those in authority, does not have to mean that the student is unsuitable. It may thus become possible for training analysts to be more ready to acknowledge that they do not necessarily always know best, and to be more open to those occasions when they could actually be getting things wrong. Therefore, when training analysts are involved in making decisions about students (or applicants) we need to be regularly mindful of the various ways in which we can, however unwittingly, get caught into some of the dynamics and problems I have tried to outline. In particular, the chairperson of any training committee needs to be much more alert to the seductiveness of 'wild analysis in committee'. He or she needs, for example, to be quick to recognize when the committee is getting into speculation, when assumptions are being made that cannot be tested, and when a student's personality is being subjected to 'wild analysis'.

Of course, what I am advocating here will not lead to more sureness about decisions in committee, for instance about students' competence, which is why we certainly need to develop much clearer criteria for qualification (as in Tuckett 2005). But, in the absence (yet) of sufficiently clear criteria, maybe it is better to remain unsure than to rely upon an illusion of sureness when that may be a self-created fiction.

Pearl King (1988) also addressed the problems that can arise when qualified analysts discover a discrepancy between how they wish to see themselves and how they actually are. She goes on to say:

> It is at such times in our professional life as psychoanalysts that we need to seek the security of a group or a water-tight theory, to compensate for our inner insecurity. This is when we are vulnerable to the innuendoes or demands for loyalty from past teachers, colleagues, supervisors or even our former training analysts. When this happens, we may find that by giving way to these pressures, we have taken up a position in relation to some important issue concerning an individual or a policy decision which on independent reflection we felt was wrong or unfair, and we realize that thereby we have compromised our integrity. In such a case we may even have been aware of the undercurrents, and felt that it was not worth risking the disapproval of colleagues by taking a different point of view.
>
> (King 1989: 346–347)

I think that there are dynamics such as those described by Pearl King which may at times lie hidden behind some decisions about students (or applicants) even when the decision is recorded as having been unanimous. This is not surprising when we remember that even training analysts are human, and as likely as anyone to be swayed by group dynamics, by such matters as loyalty to colleagues, or wishing to be thought well of by others on committees. Also, for similar reasons, it can happen that a dissenting voice in a committee is either not heard or is not adequately expressed.

The messenger or the message?

Quite a lot of what I have been trying to address in this chapter may be unpalatable. So, it could be far easier to dismiss what I am saying as being exaggerated or biased, or to question my motives in wanting to raise these issues, rather than to consider the ways in which there are important truths in what I am saying. Some people might nevertheless prefer to shoot the messenger as a way of not having to take seriously what I am saying here.

We should, of course, aim for things never to go wrong in the ways I am suggesting they sometimes do. When things are in danger of going wrong in a student's training, there should be a process of self-monitoring in each of us that could give sufficient pause for reflection, so that injustice does not happen.

Whenever some injustice could be happening, training analysts should always be willing to consider where that injustice might be, to prevent it from happening and/or to see that it is effectively remedied. Instead, we more often seem to cling to the idea that these 'so-called injustices' are only in the minds of those who 'imagine' them (i.e. any student or applicant who complains). And, again, we can always fall back on some interpretation that assumes pathology in those who are claiming that they are being unfairly treated.

Analysts can always claim to have the last word. They can also cling to the idea that those who do not agree with them, in particular anyone who discomfits them with regard to their preferred ways of thinking, must in some way be mistaken. For we can always regard anyone who does not see things the same way as 'we' do as either wilfully, or as unconsciously, mistaken or unseeing. The person who makes such interpretations of another can also claim that they know better than the other does.

So, will the message of this chapter be attended to? Are there analysts who will admit to remembering that some of what I have been saying was around for them when *they* were training, wanting then to see that this kind of thing is not allowed to continue? Will they remain true to their own experience, or have they become drawn so far into the vortex of the Society, to which they have been admitted as members, that they now do not want to rock the boat?

Finally, I believe that much depends upon how senior analysts come to think of their positions of power, in relation to the differential that I have been trying to address, if we are not to perpetuate the very problems that we may once have been subjected to in our own training. For we have an important responsibility in how we exercise the power in our training status, or in our clinical position, which our theory allows us to believe that we have, in claiming to know the other better than the other knows himself or herself.

I do not think we can wait for committees to agree upon the more formal changes in our training, which others are recommending, much as those changes are also necessary. There is an urgency for us to attend to our own part in these processes that can so readily lead to the kind of problems I have been describing. We need to start now and to do this constantly.

My caution here is then to each one of us, as we take upon ourselves the mantle of 'psychoanalyst'. We *all* need to be careful that we do not begin to imagine that we have put on the Emperor's new clothes, for it is likely that others will see through our self-deception more readily than we will ourselves. We therefore owe it to ourselves, our patients, our students and to psychoanalysis itself, that we guard against the pitfalls inherent to this privileged position that psychoanalysis tempts us to claim as our own.

Notes

1   This paper was previously published in *International Journal of Psycho-Analysis*, 2005, 86: 1143–1160. Reprinted by permission of John Wiley & Sons.
2   I have chosen, for this paper, to stay with the now less-used term 'student'. I believe this describes how candidates are *actually* regarded and treated, even though the designation 'candidate' is more appropriate to their age and standing in the world outside of their institutes. It may also be of interest that, from a search in the PEP database, I have found that the term 'student' is still used nearly twice as often in psychoanalytic journals as 'candidate'. By comparison, until 1950, 'student' was used more than five times as frequently as 'candidate'.
3   Some analysts who have taught in a university are sometimes shocked to find that their usual lectures, formerly given in their institute, are not always received with the same

placid deference that they have come to expect. The question then is not what is wrong with the university students but what might be wrong in the teaching atmosphere within their psychoanalytic institute.

4   Kernberg writes of 'legitimate authority; that is, adequate power required by his or her professional functions'. (Kernberg 1996b). Problems arise when this comes to be misused, however unwittingly, in dealings with students; especially with students in difficulty.

5   I am indebted to Gregorio Kohon for pointing out to me that, even though I first heard this saying in Germany, it probably comes from a well-known saying in Argentina: *Una interpretación, fuera de sesión, es siempre una agresión.* An interpretation outside a session is always an aggression.

Chapter 6

Imprisoned minds[1]

So that we can really engage with the otherness encountered in each of our patients, we need to maintain an open mind. But how do we achieve this when our minds tend to be filled (in our training and subsequent reading) with what we are expecting to find? I am trying to engage with this paradox, emphasizing the need to restore a position of non-certainty in our thinking in order to counter-act the imprisonment of too much sureness in our clinical work. I also consider some of those times when we need to be more sure than tentative.

A number of authors have focussed on the mental imprisonment that some patients suffer from. For instance, Sharon Hymer writes:

> The imprisoned self is a powerful metaphor in psychotherapy. Many patients describe themselves as feeling trapped, confined, or imprisoned, and strongly resonate with interpretations that mirror these sentiments.
>
> (2004: 683)

As I have said elsewhere:

> The potential of psychoanalysis is paradoxical. It can either free the mind or bind it. It can liberate creativity and spontaneity, but it can also foster compliance (particularly within a psychoanalytic training).
>
> (2002: 1)

We learn in anthropology that, if we are going to appreciate and understand the ways and customs of a culture that is different from our own, it is essential to maintain an open mind. If we fail to keep that open mind we will slip into seeing others in terms of the values and sense of meaning we have arrived at within our own life and culture. None of this will necessarily apply to those we are seeking to understand. Preconception, therefore, will always distort our attempts at understanding. What follows may then be a *mis*understanding of that otherness precisely when we may imagine that we *are* understanding it. We all know this but, in their clinical practice, many analysts allow their thinking to be dominated by the theories they feel guided by, their interpretations tending to be theory-driven rather than being a more spontaneous (and mutual) discovery along with their patients.

Without an open mind we can never truly engage with the *otherness* of an Other, even with patients. Instead we may treat similarity as if it were *sameness*, imagining that we are on familiar ground simply because we are applying understanding – and theory – that is already well known to us. This can be a defence against the experience of not understanding something that may be less familiar than we wish to assume.

All of this faces us with a challenge in psychoanalysis. Freud, in his attempt to claim for his theories the status of a science, has left us with a problematic legacy. We are, of course, much indebted to Freud for opening our eyes to the dynamics of the mind, and for much that had not been articulated before. In particular, we have learned to recognize mechanisms of defence, whereby we seek to defend ourselves from some aspect of our own minds (and being) that we may prefer to deny and disown, more readily seeing whatever it may be in others than in ourselves. Analysts are quick to point out how their patients fall into denial and projection, but they do not always remain as aware of this tendency in themselves as they had been when they had a training analyst pointing this out to them.

The more we study the theories of psychoanalysis, the more we are inclined to believe that we are joining the *cognoscenti*, a group of those who 'know'. This sense of knowing can then seem to bring many benefits. We may feel thereby that we are being protected from the discomforts of ignorance, and a sense of impotence that can link to that. Therefore, the more surely we grasp the theories that guide us, the more we may think we can apply these in our work as psychoanalysts.

Unfortunately, in applying our theories to those who seek our help, we are often transferring onto them some assumed understanding that has been 'culled' from elsewhere. This can result in a different, and largely unacknowledged, form of transference – *transference by the analyst*. We may then be interpreting from a mind-set we have trained in. Far from approaching each patient with an open mind, we are more often seeing him or her in terms of our own thinking and the rationale of whatever analytic group we feel most sustained by.

As ever we need to remain mindful of Karl Popper's caution that we may 'look away from, and not see, whatever might be dangerous to our pet theories' (see Chapter 4).

Alas, the practice of analysis seems too often to be conducted by people whose minds have been imprisoned by their training and by an allegiance to their preferred theories. It is therefore not without reason that psychoanalysis has sometimes been likened to a religion. Even though analysts most often regard religion as an indulgence, turned to by the insecure and by those who like to be told how to live and to be, analysts can themselves become caught up in this dynamic. Their own certainties also tend to set them and their likeminded colleagues aside from others who think differently.

As with religion, any claim to have the 'truth' becomes divisive. Consequently, those who do not agree with a preferred notion of truth, adhered to by those who are proponents of it, are often regarded as mistaken or as somehow lower in the hierarchy of learning than those who imagine they have largely mastered it.

There are many people who look for certainty, of whatever kind, to support and sustain them in a world that frequently confronts them with uncertainty. Some turn to religion. Others seek out a guru or a guide. Some look for an analyst who can offer them, more surely it seems than others might, ways of understanding themselves and those with whom they relate; and there is no shortage of analytic practitioners who are willing to satisfy something of this search for sureness. Some analysts can be extraordinarily sure in how they claim to understand their patients, and how they apply the theories by which they are guided in their clinical practice.

Unfortunately, any analytic practice that is based on this sureness will become self-fulfilling and apparently self-justifying. This is because there will always be ways of reading those who come to analysis, or life around them, or art and literature, in terms of the ideas that have been learned while training to become so sure. Much of this may be none other than 'wild' analysis, *making* connections between life and theory just because it is so easy to do; and it can be so seductive.

All of this is strangely ironic, as many people who seek help from an analyst are themselves people whose minds, in one way or another, have become imprisoned. They may be gripped by phobias, whereby they feel sure that there are aspects of life – or of relating – that have to be avoided, threatened by fearful consequences if they do not observe their avoidances. Or there are those who see life too literally in terms of their own (conscious or unconscious) 'connections', whose relating to others can be seriously impaired – as in those who have been traumatized by being let down by someone to whom they had been emotionally attached. They may come to believe that all attachment has to be avoided.

Equally, there are those who feel crushed by an acquired self-image. They have come to feel as if there is some 'monster' in their minds that is too much for anyone to engage with. Their history often illustrates how they have come to see themselves in this way, as when a parent or some other person has seemed to collapse or retaliate when a child has sought to engage them with states of mind that have been unmanageable to the child alone. Bion (1977: 114–115) has most aptly described the process whereby a child may be left with a sense of *nameless dread*, a result of some state of mind in the child having been experienced as if it had really become too much for anyone to engage with – and to bear.

When such a patient comes into analysis it can often happen that the analyst will, in due course, be presented with what the patient has come to think of as the 'worst' in himself. Winnicott has spelled out the need for this, if an analysis is to reach where it most needs to get. He says of this:

We must assume that both patient and analyst really do wish to end the analysis, but alas, there is no end unless the bottom of the trough has been reached, unless the thing feared has been experienced'

(1974: 105)

Much will depend on how the analyst then understands this and tries to work with it. I believe that the most convincing way of trying to engage with a patient's nameless dread, either when this is being presented or when a patient seems to be protecting the analyst from it, is to be aware of what is happening without being too quick in seeming to understand it.

The more rapidly an analyst tries to interpret a patient's assumed 'worst' in himself, the more likely it is that the patient will take from this a sense that the analyst seems to be confirming the patient's own unmanageable self-image, as if the analyst too cannot really stay with it – really engage with it. Instead, analysts may seem to be using interpretations as if to defend themselves from what the patient expects will be too much for them to bear. Therefore, being too quick to interpret – as if to understand – can seem to confirm a sense that the analyst might not be able to bear remaining in the presence of the patient's unthinkable thoughts. This 'putting into words' can itself be a defence, often not recognized as readily by some analysts as by the patient.

Trying to work with unconscious guilt is another clinical challenge, as when a patient is likely to experience an analyst speaking of this as if his guilt were a proper state of mind, immediately recognized by the analyst no less than by himself. The patient needs to be helped to see that this state of mind has resulted from *false* connections he has made, as when a hated younger sibling has suffered injury, has become ill, or has died. But if the analyst too quickly sees this connection, a patient can experience that as seeming to confirm the connection he, too, has made, as if he had really caused harm to that sibling. This is one of many times in clinical practice when I think it can be more productive if an analyst approaches an unconscious conflict from a position of *not yet understanding* it, regarding the likely connection in the patient's mind as irrational, rather than too quickly seeming to understand it. Patients need to discover a different view of themselves rather than feeling confirmed in what has become their own pathological self-image.

I believe that the only lasting change achieved in psychoanalysis, change that stands the test of time, is change that is discovered – often slowly – and grown into over time. What never seems to endure is when, however well-intended, a new way of seeing the self is imposed by an analyst or therapist in order to counteract a formerly disabling self-image, such as many patients bring into analysis.

This is why reassurance never really works. It only seems to reassure the person trying to give it. It is also why any deliberate attempt to provide a 'corrective emotional experience' is likely to bypass what most needs to be engaged with in the analysis. Instead, I stand by my belief that what *can become* a better experience is when a patient discovers an analyst who is prepared and able to stay with a patient's worst experiences, which are often relived in a process of experiencing the analyst as representing aspects of the worst in himself, and in his history. What can then be different is for a patient to find that an analyst can actually be 'there' for these most difficult states of mind, which others seem to have retreated from or to have deflected. Instead, some interpretation is experienced as an analyst's retreat from fuller engagement with the 'worst' in the patient's mind.

A useful discipline, I have found, is to monitor for the *quality* of any interpretation I have made, or of what I have in mind to say. This helps me to recognize when I could be slipping into some value judgment or implicit criticism of the patient. I try to remember that this is frequently a sign that I am tempted to deflect or bypass something difficult to tolerate. This can help me to return to the task of trying to understand something that I am experiencing as difficult, and that will take more time than is available when an interpretation is given too quickly. This internal supervision can also prompt me to stay longer with whatever the patient is presenting that is difficult to stay with.

Another discipline I try to observe is to note when I am becoming too sure. It is at such times that I am most likely to become blind to what I do not (yet) understand and how I may be failing a patient because of my sureness. It is precisely then that I try to re-establish *non-certainty*, to recover an open mind and the freedom to continue exploring – unimpeded by the shackles of certainty.

As I have mentioned elsewhere (2002: 16), I have greatly valued having it pointed out to me that in Sanskrit the word for *certainty* is the same as the word for *imprisonment*, and the word for *non-certainty* is the same as the word for *freedom.*

What I may need to stress here is that *non-certainty* is quite different from *uncertainty*, which is more to do with indecision. Rather it involves a clear choice to remain *non-certain*, which helps us to be open to what we might not expect to find. These two states of mind, which to some may sound similar, are in practice very different – with quite different consequences and clinical outcomes.[2]

So what are we to do with the certainties in psychoanalysis that can so imprison the minds of practitioners, and which in turn can threaten to imprison the minds of those who come to them? In the setting of psychoanalytic training it becomes all too clear that some recently qualified analysts are in danger of doing to their patients what has been 'done' to them. Their practice may then seem to be justified in the name of passing on something regarded as good that they feel they have received, and that may sometimes be the case. But it can also be a way of defending an idealized view of their analysts and training rather than daring to question and to challenge this. If their own minds have become imprisoned during their training, by the certainties of those who have been training them, can this really be considered a good outcome – either for themselves as clinicians or for their patients?

But, of course, there are times when we do need to be more sure, some of which I have discussed elsewhere (2009), especially in how we manage times of crisis. A necessary skill in analysis is therefore that of *discernment*, in learning to recognize when to be sure and when we really do need to maintain a state of elective non-certainty. Such times for being more sure are when an analysis is in danger of breakdown, or when there is a risk of suicide. Then we definitely need to be more sure than tentative. Likewise, when we need to preserve the analytic boundaries that are so necessary to protect a safe space in which a patient can risk being open to the analyst, and in letting ourselves recognize the ways in which a patient has been affected by some infringement of those boundaries.

However, when we are seeking to understand the minds of our patients we can only do this if we approach the task with our own minds genuinely free and open. Much depends upon this, whether an analysis is experienced as creative and enabling, or whether it devolves into a kind of brainwashing by another name. The future reputation of analysis, in the minds of those who might still consider seeking the help of an analyst, will partly rest upon how the analytic experience is reported by those who have been through the process. In particular, it may be judged by the extent to which trained psychoanalysts, in their practice and in how they write, demonstrate whether it has freed their minds – or has it imprisoned them?

Notes

1   Previously published in *The Bulletin of the British Psycho-Analytical Society*, November, 2011. Also in *American Imago*, 68(2), Summer 2011: 287–295. Reprinted by permission of the journal.
2   See also my chapter, 'Certainty and non-certainty' (2006, Chapter 11)

Chapter 7

The impact of the psychoanalyst upon the analytic process

This chapter was presented as a paper at a conference held in Sorrento in 2006. The theme of that conference 'to consider the person of the analyst in the psychoanalytic cure' raises important questions some of which I will try to comment on in this chapter.

Among the questions we need to be asking are the following

- How much is what we are calling 'psychoanalytic cure' a result of Freud's notion of bringing the unconscious to consciousness?
- Is it interpretation that brings about this cure?
- Is change brought about only, or mainly, through working in the transference?
- What part does the nature of the analyst's presence play in this process?

It can be a seductive idea to imagine that patients will benefit from good experience in an analysis or therapy. And some colleagues have felt driven to provide such good experience, for example by being especially positive or helpful in their analytic manner. Occasionally a patient may be able to respond positively to such treatment, but in my view this is both rare and unlikely to endure.

There are, of course, many good things that patients can encounter as part of the analytic work: being with someone who is professionally reliable, who listens with care and takes them seriously, who (in a sufficiently contained way) is emotionally responsive to them and who helps to make sense of experience that has not before been understood; and much else.

But when a practitioner *aims* to provide what is thought of as good experience there are usually quite serious consequences. We sometimes come across this situation in relation to patients who have been traumatized.

The impact of the analyst in relation to a traumatized patient

It quite often happens that a patient who has been traumatized draws the analyst into being witness to a detailed account of what happened that so affected him or her. As we listen to these details, we may determine that we should not repeat these experiences of trauma in how we are with the patient.

How we come to be *unlike* the traumatizing objects of the patient's inner world, however, can have widely differing implications for the patient. If we are being deliberately different, we may encourage the patient to keep the feelings most related to trauma split off from us and still referred to as 'out there,' with the result that they are not adequately worked through in the analytic relationship.

Nevertheless, despite our wish not to repeat situations of trauma in an analysis, it can happen that a patient may draw us into becoming, or we may slip into becoming, quite similar in some way to a traumatizing person in the patient's history. Strangely, however, this may even be part of the analytic process, with the analyst coming to represent the traumatizing other, and the patient relating to the analyst as to that other in the patient's past.

What then is required is a sufficient balance between the discovered *similarities*, which allow the analyst to be used to represent aspects of previous trauma, and the discovered *differences* that allow a resolution of the feelings most related to that trauma.

I have noticed, in my clinical encounters with patients, that sometimes what eventually is found to have been a 'good experience' in an analysis was not with an analyst whose aim was to be different from past bad experiences, but rather with one who had survived being used to represent the worst in the patient's internal world.[1]

It is through the analyst's survival of negative transference, sustained by a sufficient understanding of what is happening in this, and why, that the analyst's external reality, as a surviving object, can eventually be found. The patient's discovery that the analyst has not just survived 'without collapse or retaliation', as Winnicott often said, but has survived through a sufficient understanding of what has been happening in this process of transference, can then become a good and necessary experience for the patient. For it is in this real survival of the worst in the patient's mind that the object can be found to have survived beyond the patient's imagined destruction of it.

The above kind of experience can enable patients to begin to move beyond the phantasy relationships of their internal world, in which even a good object seems to be the product of the patient's own omnipotence, as when (in the patient's mind) that 'object' is being protected from all that the patient imagines could destroy it. Patients can then discover an objective reality in which the object is found to have a strength of its own, surviving in its own right rather than through the patient's phantasized protection of it.

It is at such times that I have found it useful to follow my own part in the analytic relationship, entering into what I think of as the process of *internal supervision* (Casement 1985; 1991). In the course of this, I try to monitor how a patient may be experiencing me in the session. This helps me to recognize those elements of objective reality in the analytic relationship, that are being used by the patient to represent elements of traumatic history. Or, by contrast, it can help me to recognize when a patient may be responding to something about me that might seem to indicate I could be trying to avoid difficulties in the analysis.

So, when I have slipped into some kind of re-parenting of a patient, I have noticed that a patient's responses to such a move may indicate I am being seen as needing to be regarded as a good person. I may also be experienced as inviting the patient to keep bad experiences split off from the analytic relationship.

The trouble is that unless we really understand what the patient needs to bring into the analytic relationship, and what has remained unresolved, we can never actually help him or her to get beyond the expectation that trauma will continue to be repeated. In my experience, discovering this requires of me a highly personal engagement and a considerable struggle; specifically a struggle to tolerate within myself the feelings that, for a patient, lie at the very heart of any traumatic experience.

I therefore do not believe that there can be any short cuts to genuinely good experience in an analysis. *It can only be found by the patient.* And it can only be found when a patient is ready to find it.

To that end, I believe we need to engage with whatever a patient brings from earlier traumatic experience, whatever continues to cause internal conflict, and whatever continues to affect how patients relate to themselves and to others. And, when we are dealing with a traumatized patient, I believe that we need most particularly to be there for the unresolved feelings that have been associated with earlier let-down and trauma.

If an analyst/therapist is being deliberately 'good,' a patient can feel manipulated into having good feelings for the therapist. And, of course, the analyst/therapist who is seen as good would, in the patient's mind, not warrant being subjected to those negative feelings that are directed towards others who are experienced more clearly as letting the patient down.

Therefore, when an analyst/therapist, in trying to provide good experience, seems to steer the analytic relationship away from feelings that have been most associated with trauma, it can seem to confirm those particular feelings as apparently too much for anyone. The patient is then left to carry within himself these feelings that have acquired a quality of being too difficult to manage and they are therefore still regarded as overwhelming or dangerous.

Clinical example

To illustrate what I have been saying, I will now describe some analytic work with a patient who had suffered from cumulative trauma (Khan 1963) as a result of being the unplanned last child of a mother in her early forties, his father having left the home shortly after his birth. As the family story went, the father had apparently left because of this child being 'a birth too many'. His mother then seems to have found it extremely difficult to manage on her own. In particular, she seems to have found the task of being a mother to this third child too much for her, at her age.

The patient, whom I shall refer to as Mr K, had a long history of false-self compliance, having learned to develop this in his relationship to his mother, whom he had come to see as fragile, volatile and inconsistent. He had also experienced her as getting into explosive rages, particularly if he was demanding or if he in any way displeased her.

Not surprisingly, Mr K used to monitor me for any sign which he imagined might indicate that I, too, could be disapproving of him, or be about to disapprove. He was frequently anxious about 'getting it wrong' with me, asking me such questions as:

- Had he put his wet umbrella in the right place?
- Would the couch be wet after he had lain on it?
- If my diary was in a slightly different position, was I about to tell him that I would be away?
- Had that mark on the carpet been left by him?

He made many similarly anxious enquiries. Instead of answering these questions I would point to the way in which he still expected me to become an explosive mother whenever he felt that he might be getting something wrong with me.

For a long time, Mr K tried obsessively to be a good patient, indeed a perfect patient; but gradually this changed. Instead of always avoiding my anticipated anger, he began to test me out, and in doing so he would quite often taunt me contemptuously. For instance, he started saying that I was useless as an analyst; that nothing had changed. He had been coming all this time and all he had discovered was that his analyst was no good. Another similar complaint was that he 'hadn't found *any* benefit from this analysis'.

I was careful not to defend myself against these attacks. In fact, I was also careful not to treat these as simply a matter of transference, even though I did sometimes point out to him that he seemed to be saying to me some of what he had been afraid to say to his mother. But, in addition, I said: 'Nevertheless, I also have to consider the possibility that *you might be right*. Perhaps this analysis *has* been of no use to you.' I felt it was important that I should take his attacks 'on the chin', for him to see that I could consider the possible truth in what he was saying rather than deflecting it away from myself onto his mother or his absent father.

A time eventually came when Mr K noticed that, just possibly, he *had* gained something from his analysis. After all, he wasn't still stuck with feeling that he had to be a good patient, always trying to please his analyst, as he had with his mother.

He had frequently attacked me, seeking the most hurtful ways through which he might be able to get to me, and I hadn't collapsed and I hadn't retaliated. Here I think he began to find something new in his analysis and something new in himself. He could be more directly true to how he felt with me, rather than assuming that he had to hide how he was feeling in his secret self; the self he had learned to keep so hidden from his mother.

In the third year of this analysis the following sequence occurred.

Mr K generally paid me promptly at the beginning of each month. Then, he began paying me late, having 'forgotten' to bring the cheque. I had tried to explore this along the more usual lines, saying that he might be indicating some annoyance with me through making me wait. But this did not lead to much further understanding. In any case, the late payment was only occasional.

When this began happening again, I put it to Mr K that perhaps he was daring to take risks with me that he would not usually have dared to take. Maybe he was testing to see if he could pay me in his own time, rather than in mine. Perhaps he was checking to see if he could assert himself with me in this way. But I sensed that he was still anxious as to whether this would be possible without me turning into his disapproving mother; would I too explode with anger?

Mr K thought this might be what was going on, particularly as he noticed how very anxious he became when he brought his cheque late to me. Each time he had expected me to be angry, or that he would be made to feel bad and guilty (in his own words) 'for putting me to the inconvenience of having to wait'. So it seemed that he was beginning to be able to take some risks with me. But he still felt extremely anxious about it.

A few months later, Mr K once again commented that he had forgotten his cheque. It was now two weeks into the new month. On this occasion he was surprised to notice that *this time he didn't feel at all anxious*. He didn't feel any of his usual sense of urgency to settle the account. 'I might be beginning to take you for granted,' he said. Normally he would have felt self-critical and guilty, but to his continuing surprise, *to-day* he didn't feel bad about this idea of taking me for granted.

After a pause, Mr K added that he felt he might actually be beginning to trust me to mean what I said about his need to be true to himself, rather than feeling that he had to fit in with what others might be expecting of him.

I replied that he did indeed seem to be more prepared to take risks with me, daring to believe that I might allow this rather than assuming that I would inevitably be disapproving.

Comment

I was careful to stay with what he knew to be true, that it did feel like a risk. However, I did not add any confirmation as to how I might actually feel about this, nor did I say that it was all right for him to pay me late.

Mr K then said: 'You could have raised the matter earlier, perhaps pointing out that I was late in paying and asking whether there was some problem with this.' However, he then added: 'But actually there is *no* problem about paying you. It was just that I kept on forgetting to bring the cheque.'

I replied that it was true I could have initiated some discussion of this earlier, but it was possible to see something else of importance here: as I had not commented on his lateness in paying, he had found an opportunity to arrive at this new sense of trust in his own way, and in his own time.

Mr K replied: 'Yes. If you had taken it up *before*, I would, as usual, have just been responding to someone else's initiative.'

As we looked further into this, it became clear that Mr K had been able to achieve a shift within himself. Having so often felt panicky about late payment, he now saw that I might actually value his freedom to take an initiative more than I might have valued punctual payment.

This notion seemed entirely new to him. And he came to understand, without any prompting from me, that had I tried to reassure him that his forgetting the cheque didn't matter, he might have seen this as my being just like his mother, in the sense that on one occasion she might seem to be all right about something and yet on another day she might explode about the very same thing. He never knew where he was with her. With me, likewise, he had so often had a sense of not knowing where he was. But he was able to see that this came from his own thinking rather than from anything I had been saying to him.

Mr K gradually came to realize that for a long time he had used my neutrality about his late payment to represent his mother's hidden disapproval. It was only now that he discovered that, just maybe, I was different from how he had assumed me to be. But, it had been important for him to have found this for himself rather than have me spell it out for him.

Finding good experience

I have given this brief example to illustrate what I believe to be a crucial difference between good experience that is found by the patient and *so-called* 'good experience' that the analyst may try to provide.

I think a key issue here is that when an analyst is deliberately trying to present him/herself as a 'new object' to the patient, intending to provide something good to neutralize the patient's bad experience, this manoeuvre almost inevitably bypasses the obstacles to change, which remain in the internal world of the patient's mind. This same manoeuvre can result in bad experiences not being adequately attended to. Instead, these bad experiences remain 'out there', as something from the past rather than being more fully engaged with in the clinical present. When the worst is being kept out of the analytic relationship, the analyst may at best be regarded as an exception, while the patient's view of life itself remains little changed or not really changing at all. It is a very different matter when this is being encountered, and struggled with in the immediacy of the analytic relationship.

It is only when the patient has focussed on the analyst those feelings which he or she has come to regard as most difficult, even dangerous, that they can begin to be experienced as becoming manageable; at first manageable by the analyst and, in time, becoming more manageable to the patient too.

It is here that profound change can take place, change that includes both the internal world of the patient and the objective reality of the actual relationship to the analyst. It is here that the two worlds of inner and outer reality ultimately meet. And it is here that psychoanalysis is able to facilitate change that can genuinely survive the vicissitudes of life beyond the end of analytic treatment.

Note

1   It was Langs who first drew my attention to this and my own clinical experience has amply supported that observation. (Langs 1978).

Chapter 8

Self-revelation by the analyst

Some self-revelation by the analyst is inevitable. Often this may not matter. At other times it is clearly detrimental to the analytic process. However, I wish to suggest that there are some occasions when it may be an important part of the process. I therefore think it could be useful to open up discussion on these issues.

The analyst's neutrality[1]

There are generally very good reasons for striving to maintain an analytic neutrality. As the analytic process is particularly concerned with the emerging individuality of the patient, and the patient's transferences, it is important that the analyst's own personality should not impinge upon this process. Consequently, the analyst's personal values and attitudes should not be allowed to influence the patient, which is why a non-judgmental stance has always been advocated. In addition, the effects of suggestion and of charismatic influence are equally to be guarded against.

However, we find that if an analyst remains overly blank and detached this too has an effect upon the analytic process. For instance, it is by no means natural for a patient to be invited to relate to an impassive and impersonal presence, and patients vary widely in their ability to use this strange set-up. Certainly, there are those who can adjust to the blank space provided by a classical analyst, putting into it what belongs to their past experience or to their own inner world. We can then speak of transference or of projection, with some confidence that this belongs to the unfolding process of self-revelation by the patient. But, there are other patients who sometimes relate to the analyst's blank presence by becoming stilted and remote.

When a patient is being thus detached the analyst can, of course, interpret this in terms of the patient being defensive. But what is being defended against? It may be that the patient is defending against potential transferences, fearful of encountering what might emerge into the analytic relationship. On the other hand, I believe the patient may sometimes also be defending against the bizarre reality of being with an analyst who behaves in this distant and shut-off way.

A similar phenomenon was illustrated by Harlow's well-known experiments with baby monkeys that were left with a wire-cage 'mother' which could supply milk but no affective response, and it is strange that analysts have imagined that it could be therapeutic to present themselves to a patient in a similar way. I therefore think that we have to be careful not to interpret all responses to the analyst's detachment as necessarily informing us of the nature of a patient's internal world. It may sometimes be an unconscious prompt for the analyst to reflect upon how a detached way of working may itself be affecting the patient. So, an obsessive neutrality can have adverse effects upon the analytic process.

Self-revelation by the analyst: further reasons for caution

Although I wish to consider later in this chapter some reasons for a moderate degree of self-revelation by the analyst, I wish first to consider some other reasons for caution.

There is always a risk that self-revelation by the analyst will make it difficult (or impossible) to distinguish between transference and the objective realities of the analytic relationship. If the analyst then tries to interpret the patient's responses to this as transference it is likely to be unconvincing or misleading. In addition, the patient may feel manipulated and deflected by what is revealed by the analyst, or fascinated and seduced by it. It is therefore not unusual to see derivative evidence in the patient's subsequent communications that indicate the patient is feeling anxious about the analyst's ability to contain him/herself and therefore to contain others. The patient may then become defensive in the face of this. And, if a breach of the analyst's neutrality is traumatic, it can lead to a breakdown of the analysis. Therefore, any self-revelation should be considered with great caution, and the results of it followed carefully and undefensively by the analyst.[2]

Personal questions put to the analyst

There are many different kinds and degrees of self-revelation by the analyst, as in dealing with personal questions. It is often suggested that a patient's questions should only be analysed, never answered, and there are often good reasons for this. For instance, few would challenge the value of analysing questions such as: 'Are you married?' or 'Do you have children?' These and similar questions usually point to others that cannot so easily be asked, such as: Can the analyst understand issues related to marriage? Is the analyst unattached and 'free'? Might the analyst be homosexual? What might the analyst's views be about having or not having children? Can the analyst be trusted to be available to the child within the patient? And the meanings of these questions are likely to be as numerous as there are patients. This is why it is usually more fruitful to explore a patient's reasons for asking a question than to answer it.

Mr C, an only child and a homosexual, had asked me if I had children. I had not provided him with an answer, so he formed his own ideas about the sounds he could sometimes hear in the house where I had my consulting room. He eventually assumed that I, like his mother, had an only child which he thought of as a boy. When he heard the sound of more than one child he always thought of this as another child visiting. I never confirmed or corrected these assumptions as that would have prevented him from continuing to use these noises in his own particular ways to represent aspects of his own internal world. For him I continued to be a parent with only one child, and in the transference he often regarded himself as being that child.

Unwitting self-revelation by the analyst

There are times when an analyst unwittingly reveals a self-truth that is picked up by the patient in such a way that it disturbs the analytic process. Even though we might say that the patient is using this to work through something of his/her unconscious preoccupation, it may be untimely and disruptive for this element of the analyst's personal reality to enter into the analysis just then. I can illustrate this from my first consultation with the patient I have just mentioned.

When Mr C came for his initial consultation with me, and I had agreed to take him into analysis, he asked me about parking his scooter. He observed that there was a scooter already parked alongside the path up to my door. Could he put his scooter there too when he came for his sessions?

This was my only my second training case and I was not prepared for a such a tricky question in the first meeting with my patient. I therefore failed to recognize that there might be more to this question, and that it would be better to leave it unanswered until we had discovered more of what was in it. I might have said: 'I think we need time to understand what you may be telling me in asking this question' and to have left it for the patient to bring up again at some later time, if he did.

Unfortunately, I answered his question at the level of objective reality, saying: 'I don't think you will find that there's room for two scooters there.' The patient subsequently revealed that he had interpreted my response as indicating that I was afraid of his homosexuality and that I could not allow him to be that near to me! My supervisor was not surprised by this response.

Upon reflection I have no doubt that there was, at that stage of my training, some truth about my fear of being intimately related to a homosexual patient. If I had been more aware of my counter-transference here I could have been more alert to the implications in the patient's question, and dealt with it quite differently. As it was we had to do the initial work in this analysis with my patient convinced that I was afraid of letting him be close to me, as an (assumed to be) unchanging reality rather than as a manifestation of his transference. I had unwittingly blurred the distinction between his phantasy and my reality; and it took a long time to work this through.

Another way in which the analyst can unwittingly reveal something about his/her own thinking is through an interpretation that brings into the session something that more clearly comes from the analyst than from the patient.

I once heard an analyst boast of how he had 'cured' a female patient from sleeping in her sessions with him. He had been reflecting upon the phenomenon of her sleeping in his presence and he had imagined that it represented an unacknowledged wish. He had therefore interpreted to the patient her wish to sleep with him. The patient became immediately alert and she never slept in a session again.

We might wonder how this patient had heard this interpretation, particularly as it may have revealed what had been in her analyst's mind more clearly than what had been in her own. She might therefore have heard this as evidence that he had thoughts about her sleeping with him, in which case the change in her behaviour might well not have expressed the accuracy of that interpretation (as had been assumed by the analyst) so much as her alarm at being alone in a room, lying on a couch, in the presence of an analyst who had admitted to having this thought about her.

Some questions that may be better answered

There may be some exceptions to the general rule of not answering questions. Occasionally, the reason for asking seems quite clear, as when a patient asks: 'Do you know this film/play/book?' I have known some analysts who would refuse to answer, with the explanation that it might excite a patient's curiosity about the analyst's private life, what he/she might do with leisure-time and what the analyst's interests are. Equally, if the analyst has not seen or read whatever, it might expose the analyst as uncultured or ignorant.

I have tried not answering these questions, and there are times when it is easy to be non-committal by responding with something like: 'It might help if you give me your own account.' But there have certainly been other times when a patient has felt fobbed-off, wishing to know whether it is going to be necessary to give a fuller account of some complicated story when much of it could be taken for granted if I were already familiar with it.

In my opinion, it has not been productive to have a patient exasperatedly giving the detail of a film that I had just seen, and saying: 'If you have seen this it seems an awful waste of time telling you all this.' One could wonder why a patient chooses to waste that time. Or, one might wonder why the analyst does not simply say: 'Yes, I have seen it' (or not), or 'I have not seen it (or not read it) recently so it might help if you say what you want me to know about it'.

When I have responded more naturally, patients have not usually become preoccupied to know what else I go to see. And if they are, that can be useful too. A key test is whether an analyst's response furthers the analytic process or becomes an obstacle to it.

Unsolicited self-revelation by the analyst

Sometimes an analyst might deem it appropriate to tell a patient some personal detail, thinking that it is useful or pertinent at the time. But, even though there may be some exceptions, most usually when this is unsolicited it is likely to be prompted by some counter-transference. An example might be helpful.

I try to be very careful to keep to an absolute minimum any interruption in my arrangements with my patients, giving plenty of notice of holidays and other absences. But, when a close relative died, I could give very little notice that I would be absent for the funeral.

With all my patients except two, I said: 'Next week I have to be away unexpectedly on Wednesday,' and these patients were left free to have their own ideas about why. Perhaps I was going to give a paper, and they could be angry that I was putting my own interests before theirs. Or, perhaps I was getting tired and wanted to have a day off. Or, I was angry and wanted to get my own back. Or, I might have a relative who was ill, but why didn't I go at a weekend? Or, just possibly, I might be going to a funeral. These patients were free to range from anger to concern and back to anger as they did not have any facts to inhibit that process. It was very fruitful.

I had two particular patients for whom a sudden and unexplained absence at that time might have seemed unduly callous, because of the difficulties they were each going through. I therefore varied how I handled telling them about my absence. I said: 'There is a funeral next Wednesday that I wish to attend.' These patients were both initially grateful to me for saying why I would be away. Their subsequent responses were, however, quite different. One felt I was infantilizing her, not believing that she would be able to manage an unexplained absence. The other patient complained of me being defensive (which I was being) and that I was deflecting her from responding to this absence in whatever way she might have done. She might, for instance, have been angry. But, I was told, I had now inhibited her from being angry, because she felt I might have been in a frail state because of someone important to me having died. Eventually, she was angry with me for having tried to deflect her anger. So we were able to work it through in due course, but not without problems that had been introduced by me.

I think that these examples offer a useful object lesson. I also think that it opens up a whole area of debate about which personal situations it might be helpful to explain to patients, and why. For example, when an analyst has to be absent for surgery, what should be told to patients? An analyst with a marked limp was going to be off for a while for a hip replacement. Should he have told his patients (which he did) or not? And how would one try to decide which course is right, and with which patients? One could say it would be pretty obvious why that analyst was going to be away. But what kind of burden do we give to a patient if an analyst gives that information? Any operation, particularly for an elderly person, carries some risk to life. Conversely, what might we be doing to a patient if we do not say this, particularly if an analyst has some life-threatening condition, such as cancer?

I do not think that we can formulate an approach to these problems that could apply to all patients. Instead, we can do what feels best at the time and we can monitor how different patients deal with this. We can share our experience with others so that we might learn how we might best handle these different situations. We might then get a clearer idea about when it could be appropriate for an analyst to give some personal facts and when it might be better to leave the patient the freedom of not knowing.

The problem of a patient's curiosity

There is always a risk that self-revelation may arouse a patient's curiosity, particularly if this is gratifying a wish to know personal details about the analyst. A reliable test is whether information about the analyst leads productively into further investigation of the patient's life and internal world or into a reversal of roles, the patient investigating the analyst. There are, however, two related exceptions to this that I now wish to consider.

The analyst's inscrutability as defence

Some patients have had parents who were inscrutable, or who have been defensive about others knowing their own hidden thoughts and feelings. This can create a problem for such a patient in analysis, particularly when the analyst is experienced as behaving as a parent had done. Is that to be regarded as transference? And if it is, how is a patient expected to distinguish transference from objective realities in the analytic relationship? I am convinced that there needs to be a sufficient difference between the analytic relationship and a patient's experience of primary relationships if it is going to be possible to work meaningfully on a patient's experience of transference.[3] A delightful quotation to that effect has been pointed out to me:

> If the analyst cannot be experienced as a new object, analysis never gets under way; if he cannot be experienced as an old one, it never ends.
>
> (Greenberg 1986)

Sometimes, I believe, it helps a patient to know enough of the analyst's reality to be able to recognize when it is transference that is predominating in the analytic relationship and when it is not. To that end I will occasionally give some indication that I am not entirely as the patient is assuming me to be. Again, there will always be a danger that this exposure can be seen as defensive and I always try to follow the outcome to see whether the analytic process has been enabled or deflected.

Accurate perception by the patient

Some patients who were perceptive children have often been faced with a parent's defensive or confusing behaviour when he/she had accurately perceived some element of a parent's denied reality. Such a patient might, for example, accuse the analyst of being preoccupied in a session. If that be the case, I do not think that anything is lost if the analyst simply admits this. I am not suggesting that the analyst should enter into any further self-exposure as to what that pre-occupation had been, or why in this session.[4]

But it can be a valuable affirmation if an analyst can acknowledge a patient's perception when this has been valid, particularly when parents had been unwilling to be open about their own shortcomings.

Far from getting in the way of working with the transference, an analyst's non-defensive honesty may subsequently allow a patient to feel able to make use of the analyst more freely. By contrast, when an analyst becomes defensive in ways similar to those of a pathogenic parent it is likely to create an impasse, that similarity then amounting to an actual re-enactment by the analyst of how the parent(s) had been. An analyst's anonymity may be in the name of 'good technique' but there are times when this fails some patients of the kind I am referring to here.

The analyst's differential response to projections

I find it strange that no-one seems to be concerned about the self-revelation that is regularly demonstrated when an analyst is responding to projections of 'bad' aspects of a patient's self. There is nothing neutral about saying that a patient is projecting aggression, greed, sadism, envy or jealousy, and so on, criticizing others for characteristics which the analyst can recognize as 'belonging' to the patient. True, the analyst may go on to identify how the patient has acquired this 'bad' that is being projected. But some value judgement is clearly operating here, however objective the analyst is trying to be.

By contrast, analysts often respond quite differently when a patient is pro-jecting something good that is not being recognized in themselves. The reason is usually said to be that of not gratifying the patient; that an analysis should be conducted in abstinence.[5] If it is likely to be gratifying some narcissistic wish of the patient, I agree that the analyst should not be doing that. But there may occasionally be a case for an analyst responding differently with patients who have been severely deprived of essential self-affirmation in childhood.

Some people use projection of their 'good objects' in order to protect these from being destroyed within their own internal world, felt to be dangerous, with the result that the good is attributed to others, as if for safe keeping. And some have learned to be afraid of a critical (and often envious) parent's response to any identifiable good in themselves as a child. A patient may also have experienced critical attacks from such a parent when someone else has responded positively to good in them as a child because this might show up the parent's own failure to be more appropriately affirming.

Now, when the logic of interpreting projected 'bad' is to face what is difficult to face, I find myself wondering about the same logic in relation to patients who characteristically project the good aspects of themselves. I have therefore, sometimes, deliberately confronted patients with the good in themselves that they are in the habit of disowning. But I am careful not to do this when it is likely to be inappropriately gratifying. When a patient finds it difficult to face some good thing about him/herself, I consider it to be part of the analytic work to help the patient to do so. Naturally, this also amounts to revealing that I am aware of the patient as talented, perceptive, clever, attractive, or whatever. As such it amounts to self-revelation, but I find that important work can grow from this. The test, I believe, is whether this is something that the patient needs to face, and what use (or misuse) a patient subsequently makes of such a revelation.

A patient (Miss D) had a mother who often seemed to be criticizing her for any achievement. Part of the reason for this seems to have been because the mother may have envied her daughter. She also seemed not to tolerate her daughter establishing a separate life.

This patient happened to be a talented painter, but she had kept her talent almost entirely hidden from others. What she had allowed others to see of her painting had always been different from the painting she kept private. She had, however, allowed me to see some of these private paintings in the course of her analysis.

One day, when a prestigious art exhibition was currently showing, I mentioned this to Miss D saying: 'A lot has been changing in you recently. You might one day find that you could consider offering some of your work for that exhibition.'

In saying this I was deliberately challenging my patient's habitual hiding of her creativity from the sight of others, and I did so because I knew that her customary inhibition was perpetuating a pathological relationship to her mother. Incidentally, I was also revealing that I recognized her talent in painting. Inevitably this affirmation amounted to quite a crisis for this patient, as I was confronting her with the notion that she might face an experience she had always avoided. I was also subjecting her to the pain of contrast as I was affirming her in ways that, it seemed, her own mother had not.

The aim was not to be a 'better parent'. That is usually counter-productive. The main issue was to confront this patient with something she had been avoiding for most of her life. She might then allow herself to become visible to others, in particular to allow something good about herself to be seen. The fact that I was doing what her parents had not done was incidental. This did, however, help her to make moves within herself which had previously been seriously inhibited.

Self-revelation: direct or indirect?

I believe that self-revelation by the analyst creates quite different dynamics in an analysis depending upon whether this is direct or indirect, and whether this happens deliberately or unwittingly.

There is always a much greater risk that a patient will feel manipulated by a direct expression of what the analyst is feeling. However, there may be occasions when it is appropriate for an analyst to give affirmation to a patient indirectly. For instance, there are times when a statement can be made generally which can also apply to the patient.

Miss E, an attractive patient, regularly assumed that I regarded her as physically 'repulsive', which was how she interpreted my analytic neutrality. For quite a long time I had thought that she was manipulating me for compliments, and if she had been I would not have given that. But her assumption here pointed to a far-reaching problem, in that she interpreted much of her experience in terms of her distorted self-image.

In following the transference here, I learned that she had imagined her father had seen her as repellent, mainly because he had started being remote from her just when (aged four) she was becoming particularly attached to him. Her mother seems to have been repressive and disapproving. So this patient had formed a view of herself in a home atmosphere in which she felt her sexuality had been regarded as bad and possibly dangerous.

Having tried most other ways of shifting these negative assumptions about herself, I one day offered the general comment: 'A father should be able to see his daughter as attractive, even as desirable, without having to possess her.' This patient had previously seen an analyst who had shown too much overt interest in her, so I added: 'And the same should be true of an analyst.'

We could argue about the wisdom of making such a statement to a patient. However, I had so far failed to shift her negative self-image. Here, I hoped that my more direct statement might convey enough of my feelings to help her to shift beyond her fixed transference assumptions about me and about herself in relation to me.

Another patient, often preoccupied with suicide, had been speaking of an over-eater known to her who was threatening to walk out of therapy. I recognized the allusion to my patient's wish to walk out of her analysis in order to kill herself. Instead of interpreting this again, as I had often before, I simply said: 'What a waste.'

The next day my patient said, 'I know that you care. You said "what a waste" about that other person and I know that you feel the same about me. That is why I can't commit suicide. It would be so much easier if I felt sure that you didn't care.'

I believe that my response had more impact upon my patient because it had been a spontaneous expression of my feelings, about someone in a parallel situation to her own. It was certainly more effective than any direct declaration of caring for my patient, which could have been dismissed as manipulative. But my patient was able to get a sense of my caring for her because it had been offered obliquely, and this had a lasting effect. Her own parents seemed to have shown little or no caring for her that she could remember.

Self-revelation through counter-transference

I wish to consider counter-transference here in different ways.

Foremost, an analyst needs to monitor any strong feelings about a patient in order to contain those from deflecting the process of an analysis. In addition, counter-transference may also serve a diagnostic function whereby the analyst is helped to recognize something important about the patient.[6]

Miss E (described above), had registered something of what I said about fathers and analysts but she continued to think of herself as unattractive. Further work was necessary to shift this paralysing conviction.

Later in the analysis, there was a period of a few weeks during which I made a number of mistakes about time, all relating to this patient. It happened that I had suppressed the fact I had pressed the door-opener for this patient while I was engrossed on the telephone, with the result that Miss E was left a long time in the waiting room while I appeared to be unaware that she had arrived. And twice I ended a session five minutes early. I was clearly enacting some counter-transference here. I was naturally troubled by my repeated mistakes, and I could not hide from myself that these were specific to this patient.

When I examined my thoughts and feelings around this I realized with quite a shock that I had been shutting out my feelings for this patient because I found her attractive. My 'neutrality' with her had therefore become stiff and I had been maintaining an exaggerated distance as my way of not getting too close to her, bearing in mind that her previous analyst had alarmed her by being too friendly. My stance was then tantamount to a reaction formation against being attracted to her, which had led her to see me as (apparently) being repulsed by her.

I had concealed my positive feelings about this patient, but they had become evident despite myself. It was also possible that my reaction against finding her attractive may have echoed something from her experience with her father. His love for this child, expressed in a natural physical closeness, seemed to have stopped suddenly when she began to show a strong Oedipal attachment to him. He had then become distant from her with the result that she had come to see herself as repulsive to him, as to me in the transference.

Under these circumstances, I felt that this patient might be better helped if I shared with her some of my understanding of this, despite what Heimann says. She could then begin to see that my mistakes made a different kind of sense, which she had not been able to understand while she still assumed that I regarded her as unattractive.

Communication by impact

There are times in an analysis when it is supremely important that difficult feelings can really be communicated to the analyst. This is especially true when a patient is using communication by projective identification. The patient then needs to find some evidence that this has not only reached the analyst but is having an effect upon him/her. When an analyst is truly in touch with difficult feelings they will be experienced as difficult. Often it is the evidence of emotional contact that counts more than a clever interpretation.

A patient who had been telling me about an experience that had been very important to him, noticed my expression at the end of the session. The next day he referred to this, saying that he knew I had shared the experience. This had meant a lot to him as he had not been able to share difficult feelings with either of his parents.

Notes

1   Gerard Franklin has provided a valuable discussion of the issue of neutrality in his paper 'The multiple meanings of neutrality' (1990) in which can also be found a full and useful review of the literature.
2   Langs (1978 and elsewhere) has given many examples to support the idea that self-revelation by the analyst will always be detrimental to the analytic process, but I do not believe this to be universally true. I am therefore wishing to reflect upon times when other considerations should also be taken into account.
3   I have examined this problem elsewhere, in 'The experience of trauma in the transference' (Casement 1900 Chapter 5; also 1991 Chapter 15).
4   In her paper on counter-transference, Heimann states her caution about self-revelation by an analyst. The work of self-analysis 'is the analyst's private affair, and I do not consider it right for the analyst to communicate his feelings to his patient.' (Heimann 1950: 84).
5   Fox (1984) has pointed out that analysts seem to fall into two categories, the 'frustraters' and the 'gratifiers'. He goes on to argue that there should be a balance between these two positions that is more applicable to the individual patient.
6   I discuss this more fully elsewhere (Casement 1985 Chapter 4; 1991 Chapter 4).

Chapter 9

Keeping in mind[1]

At various times in an analysis the analyst/therapist may say to a patient, as before an absence or at a time of particular distress for the patient, 'I will keep you in mind'. It may be that we intend to do just what we say, but do we really? I think that we should keep our patients in mind, even without promising to do so. And, at times, this can turn out to have been crucial.

A suicidal patient[2]

A patient I will here call Miss G was someone who had been referred to me by a psychiatrist after she had made a serious attempt at suicide. She had been seeing me once a week for a year, attending every session and arriving exactly on time or, sometimes, early. But she never once came late.

I have long believed that I should start each session on time, *with or without the patient*, thus spending the first part of the session, at least, wondering what the lateness or absence might mean.

One day Miss G was not there for her session. What might have happened? She might have been held up by traffic. But, if not, then why was she not there for her session?

What should I do about this? I was at first reluctant to telephone as that could be experienced as intrusive. Then I found myself recalling the beginning of this therapy, that it had been after a serious overdose. So, might Miss G be back with that suicidal drive?

I began to feel that I should phone. It would not matter if she were delayed on the bus as, in those days, there was no automatic registration of the caller's number.

When I did phone, her number was engaged, and continued to be engaged every time I rang. I then began to feel that she might have left her phone off, perhaps deliberately, especially as this was during her session time and she might have guessed that her therapist would, most likely, phone. I then managed to contact the telephone exchange, which was possible in those days, and asked for the number to be checked to see if it was 'engaged speaking' or just 'off the hook'. They confirmed that it was off the hook. So, I asked to be connected to the phone so that I could call out. I called Miss G by name, loudly and repeatedly, getting no response. I then phoned the GP immediately and told him that I believed there was a serious risk that Miss G had taken another overdose. Could he please arrange for her to be visited, immediately? This he did, and Miss G was found unconscious, having taken an overdose that could have been fatal. If I had not kept her in mind, she could have died.

I see this example as a valuable reminder that we should always consider possible communication in behaviour and, as here, in lateness.

Two minutes late[3]

I was seeing a patient who was exceedingly compliant, always wishing to please, and (to my shame) it was he that I first asked to change a session time, so that I could find a fifth session time for my second analytic training case. He had, without hesitation, said that would be OK. However, when we came to his next session, the patient was not there. On wondering about this I recalled that this patient, like Miss G, had never ever been anything but exactly on time or early. So, what might this lateness or absence be telling me?

As it happened, he arrived within two minutes of his session time, so maybe there was nothing much in this. But, the more I thought about it during the session, I began to feel uncomfortable about my having taken advantage of this patient's habitual compliance and his constant wish to please.

So, later in the session, I said to him that I was thinking about his unusual lateness in arriving for his session. I then commented that I was familiar with his not complaining, even when people had taken advantage of him, and I now felt that I had quite wrongly exploited his tendency to please. Perhaps, in his two minutes' lateness there was a whisper of complaint about that change of session time. He didn't disagree, so I added that I was taking seriously his complaint and I thought we should keep to his usual session times, without that proposed change. He seemed quite moved by this and that is how we continued. His complaint had been heard.

An adopted child[4]

Miss J, as I shall call her, was referred to me for analysis when she was about eighteen. She first saw me just a few weeks before I would be taking my Easter break. She struck me as very fragile. I learned that she had been adopted, but also that things had begun to get out of hand in her adoptive home. The father seemed to have fallen in love with her, so she felt she had to leave the home in order to find somewhere that might feel safer for her than her home seemed then.

I did not think that it would be right to start immediately in five times a week analysis, only then for her to be immediately abandoned by my going away, nor did I think she should be made to wait until I got back from my holiday.

I therefore suggested that she came once a week for the three weeks left before the break and that we could start her analysis when I returned.

It so happened that I had long chosen to keep my dress, for clinical work, as consistently the same; always the same tie and (usually) a brown jacket. So, Miss J had seen me each time as always dressed the same way. But, during that Easter break, my wife had convinced me that I could no longer continue to wear that brown jacket as it was splitting down the back and I would have to get a new one. I could not find another brown jacket, so I had bought a blue one.

About three months into her analysis, Miss J confessed to feeling acutely anxious and insecure, also confused. 'Where is the man in a brown coat?' she asked. I didn't at first understand what she was asking me. She then explained that she had been referred to someone who had agreed to see her, a man in a brown coat. But then, after the Easter break, she had found herself landed with someone completely different, someone who wore a blue coat.

As we explored this confusion it became clear that Miss J had experienced the change of coat as representing a change of person seeing her, just as she had found herself moved from her foster parent to the adopting parents. It felt as if she had, again, been passed over to a stranger without her permission or understanding. Her experience of adoption had come to be experienced as being repeated in the analysis, now alive in her experience of me.

A prolonged absence

Later in Miss J's analysis, interestingly also during an Easter break, she wrote to me to say that she was working as a nurse on a kibbutz, where she felt valued, and she wished to stay longer. Would I please keep her session times for her until she got back? She would definitely pay for her missed sessions upon her return. I readily agreed to this.

After a month of this prolonged break Miss J wrote again. She again wished to extend her absence. Would I please continue to keep her session times until she returned, and she repeated that she would pay for the time missed. Again, I agreed.

Now, following my practice of starting each session on time, with or without the patient, I continued to observe each of Miss J's session times by moving my diary from behind the couch, where it was for most of my time, to be by the chair I used for patients who were being seen face to face. By the time Miss J had begun to be away I had been seeing her face to face. So that was where I placed my diary, for every one of her missed sessions.

I did not hear further from Miss J until, after three months' absence, she rang the patient's bell and she arrived to find me sitting ready for her, as I had been for every session she'd been away.

This had a most profound impact upon Miss J. I had *really* kept her in mind, for all the time she'd been away. I have since shuddered to think of the effect if

I had forgotten her or, worse still, if (like some analysts) I had filled her time with another patient.

A gift was offered

After Miss J had resumed her analysis, we came to the next Christmas break. She wanted to give me a present, and came shyly offering this to me. It was an exquisitely carved book-marker. I responded by saying: 'Gifts can complicate an analysis, so I am wondering how best to deal with this now. I don't want you to feel hurt or rejected if I were to hand the intended gift back to you. I also don't feel it would be quite appropriate for me to accept it straight away as a present. Instead, I would like to suggest that I keep it here, by my chair as *not yet a present*. Then, when we come to the time when you are leaving here, we can think again about this.' When that time came, a year or two later, I still had the gift there beside me. I reached for it and said to her: 'This is when we need to make a decision about who keeps this beautiful book-marker.' She firmly said she wished it now to be her gift to me. I replied that I would remember her anyway, even without this, but I would also continue to treasure the gift.

I still do. And the book-marker is still on the shelf by my chair – some twenty years later.

Notes

1   First published in *The Bulletin of the British Psycho-Analytical Society* (2018, 54(2)). Republished by permission. This paper is a commissioned chapter to be included in *'Out of hours': between boundary attunement and a paradigm shift in psychoanalysis and psychotherapy* (in press, 2019), (eds.) Sinason, V. and Sachs, A. Routledge: London.

2   Another version of this example was published previously in *Learning from life* (2006, Chapter 3).

3   Another version of this example has been published previously: 'Between patients' in *Between sessions & behind/beyond the couch*, (ed.) Joan Raphael-Leff (2002). London: Karnac Books.

4   This example is also contained in the paper (Raphael-Leff 2002) just quoted.

Chapter 10

Beyond words

The role of psychoanalysis[1]

My aim in this chapter is to consider some of the ways in which problem-focussed therapies such as cognitive-behaviour therapy (CBT) may be attractive, but also some of the ways in which these therapies may in the long term fail to provide the relief that is most deeply being looked for. Patients frequently need time to achieve an enduring resolution to their inner conflicts. They must discover solutions within themselves rather than, as in some cases, having superficial solutions imposed upon them by someone who is aiming for quick results in order to satisfy those who are funding the therapy.

CBT as an attractive therapy

It can indeed be very appealing to think that here is a form of therapy that can be both brief and effective, and in some cases I believe it may be. When compared to psychodynamic therapies, CBT may seem to be much cheaper, so it will of course be attractive to a provider. It may also be closer to what many people believe they are looking for, in being given practical advice and being taught strategies for managing difficult situations. It may appeal to common sense more readily than do the mysterious theories and practice of psychoanalytic therapy. And it may seem to produce results that are more amenable to being measured than are the results from psychoanalysis or psychotherapy.

But what about people who come back for more treatment? For example, in the long term, CBT may not always be cheaper when consideration is given to those patients who seek further help because the coping strategies provided for them have not adequately resolved their underlying conflicts.

From the position of any psychoanalytic practice we are bound to wonder about the effectiveness of a therapy that aims to suppress or change symptoms rather than to understand them. We are also concerned that there may be more trouble later from what is being suppressed or changed, and from what may remain unconscious, as symptoms are often an expression of unconscious conflict that is seeking resolution. So what may happen when the unconscious communication in symptoms is pushed aside in favour of some more immediate relief?

Unconscious communication and monitoring of clinical process

Some communication is not deliberate and is beyond one's own awareness. It may however convey some unrecognized intention, as in forgetting an important appointment. Similarly, it may signal the presence of conflict that one may not be aware of, as in a slip of the tongue that indicates a hostile wish one may consciously want to conceal. Much unconscious communication is nonverbal, as in behaviour indicating unmet needs, for instance behaviour that conveys the need for someone to engage with difficult feelings or with a state of mind that has come to be regarded as unmanageable by others.

For monitoring the psychotherapy process, I have relied a lot on a clinical discipline I call *internal supervision* (Casement 1985; 1991). This is how I have come to monitor my own work and the clinical work of those who present to me in supervision or in clinical seminars.

An important part of this internal supervision is trial-identifying with the patient in the session. This helps me to follow my own part in the clinical process, considering from the viewpoint of the patient how they may be experiencing my input into a session.

Another part of internal supervision is to look for unconscious prompts from the patient that can help me to recognize when a patient is being affected by me in ways that I had not meant, and had not anticipated.

For example, patients quite often give unconscious criticism of the therapist. Someone else may be spoken of as not understanding, or as avoiding something difficult, perhaps indicating that this is how the therapist is being perceived. Or a patient may speak of someone else who really addresses something difficult, as if to say to the therapist and why don't you?

Staying with what is difficult or by-passing it

I have frequently noticed that patients show more than one level of response to what is being presented to them. Perhaps the easiest example of this is when we fall into giving some form of reassurance to a patient in distress.

We might, for instance, be wanting to help a patient to see that things will get better even though at the moment that may seem very close to impossible. At one level a patient might show signs of gratitude that we seem to be helping them to get beyond their current sense of hopelessness. But, at another level, it often becomes apparent that a patient sees the therapist as backing off from what is most difficult for the patient.

A simple example of that may be before a break from therapy, as for a therapist's holiday. A patient may *seem* to manage, but they often show signs, if we can let ourselves notice them, that this coping has been at a cost. A patient may speak of no one recognizing their state of distress, which could include the therapist. Patients also monitor to see if the therapist is willing to remain close to their inner states of mind.

I have often found that patients feel better held through a break when they sense that the therapist is willing to remain in touch with how shaky they are actually feeling. If patients are encouraged to step aside from their inner insecurities, in order to appear to be coping while the therapist is away, they are left even more alone with their deepest fears.

Some particular states that may not be helped by CBT

CBT therapists are often giving their clients strategies for coping, which may be helpful to some, but there are many patients who need something much more than this.

An example comes to mind when I was seeing a patient with bulimia (Casement 1985, Chapter 9; also 1991 Chapter 9). She had already received 'a belly full' of advice from all those with whom she had close personal dealings with regard to her compulsive eating. She had received frequent diet advice, drug therapy (antidepressants and appetite suppressants) and behaviour therapy. Eventually she had been made to have her jaws wired. All of this had failed. What, in the end, had the most potent therapeutic effect upon this patient was her realization that I had never tried to guide her or to tell her what to do, or what not to do. This had been the first time in her life that she had been in a relationship of this kind, a freedom being preserved for her in which she could begin to discover 'her own version of herself'. This phrase became a mantra that she frequently referred to. And it was this in particular that she took away with her after seeing me for about fifteen months.

This patient called on me ten years later. She wanted me to hear and see how she had thrived since she had stopped coming to see me. She was clear that she had found in the analysis something that had been uniquely different from all other kinds of help that had previously been thrust upon her. Only in her analysis had she found a freedom to become herself.

Another kind of patient who will not be helped by CBT is the kind that has come to be known as 'false-self' (Winnicott 1955). These have come to feel that they have to satisfy significant Others in their lives by being good, by being compliant, by not being themselves. These patients, unlike the patient above, may seem to thrive upon being given advice, being offered strategies for coping. But all of this may only add to their problems about being real, in not daring to confront others, not daring to be as they feel.

Another group that may not be helped by CBT are some traumatised patients for whom the principal trauma has been internal. This can happen when a breakdown in relationship has been associated with a sense that a significant Other has not been able to bear the intensity of a patient's feelings and/or neediness, or indeed their own aliveness, most particularly during early childhood. (cf. Bion 1967: 114–115). As a result, patients may feel that they have to protect any significant Other from whatever is now thought to be too much for anyone.

These patients, if they are to get beyond this compulsion to protect their significant Others from all that is most alive in themselves, need eventually to be able to bring all that has been most dreaded in themselves into an ongoing, present day relationship, as with an analyst or therapist. They then need to be able to discover that this therapeutic Other is able to survive, without collapse or retaliation, all that had previously seemed to be dangerous, even lethal, if not kept away from a significant Other. Only then, and gradually, may they begin to realize that they can allow themselves to be more fully alive, more free to engage others intimately, not having to remain fearful of their anger or their hate, their dependence upon others or indeed their own aliveness (Winnicott 1971).

This kind of work cannot, in my opinion, be engaged with in CBT, especially when a premium is being set on the length of therapy. Also, if we monitor a patient's responses to the therapist's style of working, we are likely to find that patients are having their deepest fears seeming to be confirmed, that this person too seems to be avoiding the worst in their mind. Even though that worst in them may come to be better concealed as a result of CBT, it is not going to be detoxified. The unconsciously assumed qualities of all that is being avoided will then seem to have been too much for the therapist to manage.

Much takes place in therapy that lies beyond any matter of learning strategies for coping. There is much also that lies beyond words: that is beyond what a patient is able to speak about, and beyond what a therapist is addressing with words. If we are not going to fail our patients we often need to tune into the deeper significance of this, in symptoms, in behaviour, in avoidance, in tone of voice, in body language and manner. We need to monitor each party in the therapeutic relationship for the communication that lies beyond words. For it is here that we can discover how extensively some patients are affected by what they perceive in their therapists, whether the therapist is willing and able to stay with the deepest distress in their minds or whether the therapist is behaving in ways that are seen as an avoidance of that.

Note

1   Previously published in *The Psychologist*, May 2009, Vol 22: 404–405. Reprinted by kind permission of the journal.

Chapter 11

Art therapy[1]

This chapter is based on an address given when I was invited to be a keynote speaker for the Goldsmith's Conference 'Finding spaces and making places,' April 2016, alongside Grayson Perry, who was the other keynote speaker.

Grayson spoke first, walking up and down while he spoke excitedly to a PowerPoint presentation of impressive slides. I knew I could not compete with that, so I abandoned what I had planned to say and spoke off the cuff. The text here was transcribed by Dr Robin Tipple, of Goldsmith's, from a video that was made at the time.

First, where have I come from and how do I come to be here?

My name is Patrick Casement. I had hoped that there might be some copies here of my latest book (2006) which describes something of the circuitous journey I travelled as I struggled to free myself from my family's wish to get me to go into the Royal Navy like all the male members of my family, three generations of them. As you can see, I got away.

So here I am, and I know nothing about Art Therapy. I know a lot more about being a bricklayer's mate, that being my first job after having graduated. After that I trained as a social worker, then as a psychotherapist, and I subsequently trained again to be a psychoanalyst. That's the official account of my CV. There is, however, another version of that, which came to me from somebody who had asked my mother, years ago: 'What is Patrick doing now?' She hadn't got a clue, even though we had been in regular contact. I was told she had replied that she knew I'd been a social worker, but she believed I was then working as a *physio*therapist. Further, I was told that she'd gone on to say: 'I gather he's training all over again, I don't know why, but I believe he's *training to be a psychotic*.' So here I am, with all those qualifications, now trying to think about this thing called Art Therapy.

The very first time I met an art therapist was fifty-five years ago and, for reasons I shall shortly explain, it was for me transforming. This experience changed things for me because I had been to see a friend's daughter who was in a psychiatric hospital. For some reason that I didn't understand, the therapist she was seeing, knowing I was training to be a psychotherapist, thought I might like to see her artwork. I now feel a bit worried about the boundaries here, but I'm pleased it happened. I was shown four images, each one of which had a big mess in the middle enclosed within some kind of circle. And from the circle were two lines going right off to the edge of the frame. The art therapist said this was because the patient had been prematurely separated, emotionally, from her mother. 'She's now trying to re-find the umbilical cord.' I thought how extraordinary. All my life I had been trying to get free of mine!

And why was this so transforming for me? It introduced me to what I now call the *otherness of the other*.

One of the things that we all tend to do, quite naturally, when we are listening to somebody who is telling us their story, is we try 'putting ourselves in their shoes'. But there is a problem about this. Very often that's *exactly* what we do. We put *ourselves* in their shoes and start reading their life experience as *we* might have experienced it, which overlooks the most essential thing: that we are not that person and that person's experience might be completely different from ours. So the *otherness of the other* is what I took away from that encounter fifty-five years ago; my first encounter with an art therapist.

I later came across some of the shortcomings in the practice of psychotherapy when I came across some psychotherapists who had no time for Art Therapy. I was taking part in a clinical discussion in America and the patient wouldn't speak. She was anorexic, we were told, and the therapist was getting frustrated. The patient then asked if she could draw. The therapist replied: 'This is a talking cure. We don't do drawing.' So that was the end of that, as far as that patient was concerned.

Sometime later I was in Japan when I was present at another clinical seminar, in which a therapist described her work with an eight-year-old girl. There was something she could not speak about. If she did it would get her father into trouble. He would be sent away from home. She couldn't speak about it, but she would be able to put it into a drawing. Again, I heard a patient being told that drawing would not be allowed in her therapy. But, if she wished, she could be referred to an art therapist. I think that was a terrible let-down for that child. And we can probably imagine the kind of thing she may have been trying to communicate. But, let's remember, without the aid of her drawing we should not assume that we know what it was about her father that she could not put into words. It was such a pity that she was not allowed to use paper and crayons as part of her ongoing therapy.

Now, for a moment, let's think about *why do we interpret?* I believe that, too often, we interpret to demonstrate a degree of what we want to think of as 'competence'. I don't know how much it's true of art therapists but it is certainly true of us psychoanalysts. I think it's because too many of us listen for a topic to which we can attach an idea, so that we can use some theory, or some under-standing, which actually comes from elsewhere. In doing so we may appear to understand, or imagine that we understand. I think that very often we are merely touching upon something we can use to demonstrate our knowledge of psycho-analysis. But that doesn't always mean we have been truly listening to the patient. Instead we may have been listening for something we can comment on. It may also be true in Art Therapy, but I don't know. So that's one idea, one question I would like to leave you with: *why do we interpret?*

Another idea I'd like to leave with you is the idea of a *'monster in the mind'*. I think that sometimes people experience themselves, in some way, as being too much for anyone, if they become too demanding or too dependent. What-ever it might be, very often they read the other person's responses as indicating what they are able, or not able, to cope with in what the patient needs to communicate. I think this sometimes develops into what I now call a 'monster in the mind'.

For instance: I had one patient who was referred to me after she had previously been to see a psychotherapist who went psychotic, and then she had been to an analyst who died of cancer. In the background was a mother who would not tolerate any demands on her. I was told that the mother used to say: 'If you go on like this, you will drive me crazy,' or 'If you go on like this you will be the death of me.' Then, in those two attempts at therapy, the first therapist had gone crazy and the second had died. So, with me, the patient had become terrified of ever being needy or demanding of me. What might that do to me?

She unconsciously assumed she had to protect me. This patient hadn't protected the therapist who went crazy and she hadn't protected the analyst who had died. So, she seemed to be protecting me all the time.

One day I said to this patient: 'I think I've come to understand something that is going on here ... There's something that you are not bringing into your relationship with me ... I'll explain, in a moment, what I am about to say. *I think that you are using sun magic.*'

She of course said, 'What?'

I replied, 'Yes. If I imagine the sun will rise each day *only* if I go through the rituals of sun magic, I may come to think that, every day, the magic seems to work. But what if I didn't do the rituals? Maybe the sun would never rise again.' And I think that the sun magic she was using with me was in not being demanding, not bringing to me any of the neediness she had associated with her mother's reactions, and the responses of her therapist and her first analyst. I therefore think that she had developed a view of herself as having some kind of monster in her that would be too much for anyone, and somehow this assumption had come into her relationship with me.

Some time ago I was supervising an experienced therapist, who was then seeing a very disturbed patient who had become exceedingly dependent upon her. Around the time I started supervising this case, the therapist was about to go abroad for a couple of months. As she was feeling very concerned for this patient during that absence, it was arranged that the patient could go to see an art therapist, temporarily, who offered to contain her while the ongoing therapist was away.

During that 'baby-sitting' period with the art therapist, the absent therapist began to receive increasingly alarmed communications from the art therapist, who was afraid the patient might be going mad. It turned out that the patient was drawing images of such gross violence, of cut-up babies and dismembered bodies, the art therapist was getting really alarmed by this. She began to think she could not cope with what was being brought to her, and she was very relieved when the ongoing therapist came back and could take over.

In supervising this psychotherapist, I came to sense that what her patient had been taking to the art therapist was what she was not bringing into her relationship with my supervisee. I felt sure that, somehow, a way had to be found to allow all that split-off violence, and near psychotic disturbance in the patient's internal world, to be bought into the psychotherapy relationship, rather than being kept apart from it. And that is what happened.

What followed was a most disturbing and terrifying series of sessions with this patient, and not only sessions; the patient also followed these up, between sessions, with letters, many of them.

Eventually, the therapy was profoundly successful and the patient later persuaded her therapist to write it up, because she felt that the overall sequence had been of such value, in having had the re-parenting thing which hadn't really touched any of the 'real stuff,' then having her experience of art therapy, and ultimately having all that violent stuff coming into her relationship with my supervisee.

It had been crucial that the therapist and I, together, had somehow managed to *hold* the patient throughout that long clinical sequence, so that the monster in the room could be managed, contained and understood, over time. With that, the patient began not to be the crazy person she had believed herself to be. That was why she later persuaded the therapist to write up this experience, her two therapies: both therapies being with the same therapist, the change-over having been the result of supervision being sought and found.

So that book is soon coming out. Its working title was *Beyond re-parenting,*[2] and it includes something of the patient's time with the art therapist, including the patient's comments on art therapy which are also extremely interesting, and valuable.

Because the art therapist, in order to survive, had kept on trying to make sense of it all, and had kept on trying to interpret, the patient said to her psychotherapist (and I quote from an early draft of the book) 'I wish she (the art therapist) wouldn't interpret. I don't *need* her to interpret. She is *only* interpreting for herself. I just need her as a witness. I need someone to witness what I am carrying in myself and for them to be able to bear it; and she can't bear it, which is why she keeps interpreting.' I thought that was a really useful bit of feedback which is why I bring it in here.

So, why do I think these things are so important? I just wish that forty years ago I'd the experience I have now, because when I first started as a therapist I had a very disturbed patient come to me who had an extremely complicated relationship with her father. That patient had brought to me a painting which, she said, represented how she imagined her father saw her. It was a truly horrifying image.

I know that you have ways of looking after images that people you work with create in your presence. They can leave the images with you. So it would seem to be the most natural thing for my patient to have hoped that I would look after the image she'd brought to me. Alas, I didn't have the experience I have had since then.

By the end of that session she got up to go, leaving the image on the table between the chairs. I said: 'I think this belongs with you.' I *wish* I had not said that, because I know she and I had never properly engaged (together) with that image. We had never properly worked with it, and there was so much work to be done on it.

Soon after, this patient stopped seeing me, and she went to another therapist. I don't know what happened there, but I do know that a few years later she committed suicide. I don't think I *caused* her suicide but I regret terribly that I wasn't in a position to grasp that opportunity when she brought it to me, to have really worked with it, and it might have made a significant difference. That's why I think these things are important.

Thank you.

Notes

1   Robin Tipple kindly gave permission to use his transcript from *Art Therapy On Line* (ATOL), 8(1) (2017).
2   This is now published as Shmukler, D. (2016). *Supervision in Psychoanalysis and Psychotherapy*. London: Routledge.

Chapter 12

The case of 'Mrs B' (my burned patient) continues to challenge

Obviously I have an investment in how I handled the case of Mrs B. Most important to me has been what I learned from following the process of that analysis. At the time, I would have much preferred not to have followed the process, and yet this analysis taught me more than any other. So I continue to hope that, even now, others might still learn something from it too.

For readers not familiar with this case, I give here a brief résumé, before proceeding to my discussion (below) of Pizer's review of my book *Learning from Our Mistakes* (2006). This can provide some background to the issues most in contention.

The patient, Mrs B, had nearly died of burns when she was eleven months old. What we did not know until near the end of this analysis was that her mother had been instructed by a doctor, after the burning, that she must only barrier nurse her baby: *she must never hold her.*

A major focus in the analysis was around a later occasion concerning not being held when, at seventeen months, Mrs B had to be operated on by a surgeon under a local anaesthetic. During this, her mother was holding her hand. Then she fainted. Mrs B had imagined that it had been her fierce need of her, when she was so intensely anxious, that had been too much for her mother, even that she might have 'killed' her when she disappeared from sight.

In her analysis, when Mrs B began to re-experience that moment with the surgeon, and then her mother no longer holding her, she had virtually demanded that I should allow her to hold my hand *if it ever got so bad again.* At first I agreed. But almost immediately Mrs B reverted to her conviction that she would have to protect me. She felt that I would collapse if it became too much for me. She sensed, quite correctly, that my offer to hold her hand would be easier for me, too, bypassing the worst that was still to be faced by allowing focus to be concentrated on the mother who had not been able to hold her.

When I consulted with Dr Paula Heimann on this, she agreed with me that I would have to find a way to withdraw the offer of my hand. In the very next session, Mrs B had an image of me as stationary, again controlled by her. She saw me becoming a collapsed analyst. It was then that I knew I must withdraw the offer of my hand, a clinical decision that several commentators have failed to understand.

Some commentators have suggested how much better they would have handled this sequence in the analysis. They have argued from what seemed to them to have been a more humane stance under the circumstances. Unfortunately, some commentators had only been aware of the first published account (1982), not the later account (2002) in which I give the corroborative facts (repeated below) that were only later revealed by Mrs B's mother.

Perhaps these commentators had not learned much from this case. In contrast, I have learned from it some most profoundly important things about the potential in psychoanalysis.

During most of this analysis, neither Mrs B nor I knew anything about the long period of *barrier nursing after the burning*. We learned of it only after she had told her mother about her analysis, during which it had become possible for her to get beyond her worst fears of being too much for anyone she depended on. This had only become possible as a result of her analyst *not* holding her but still being there for her feelings about not being held.

She had told her mother that her analyst had been able to bear being the focus of all she had felt when her mother had withdrawn her hand. The analyst had continued to be there for her even when she had focussed all of her anxiety and rage on him. He had been able to bear all of that and had not collapsed. It was only then that her mother felt able to share her own terrible experience of having to barrier nurse her baby through weeks and months of pain. Only then had her mother felt able to speak of her own almost unimaginable distress at not being allowed to offer natural comfort by holding her baby.

The pressure Mrs B initially put upon me had me enacting the possibility of her holding my hand, whilst her unconscious prompts indicated immediately that she'd begun to see me as a collapsed analyst. This it was that led me to withdraw that offer of holding her.

Only later could we see the *screen memory* function that had been active during our work around her not having her mother's hand to hold. That screen memory kept us focussed on the later not holding until Mrs B could be more able to face what lay behind it: that other unimaginably intolerable period of not being held during the barrier nursing, of which she had no conscious memory until her mother told her those earlier details.

I remain convinced that this analysis went the way it did because I followed my patient's most unwelcome prompts and also because of her courageous persistence. I also gladly accept Mrs B's own validation of the route taken by the process, for which she has told me she has remained profoundly grateful.

Much can be lost when a challenge such as we find in this case is dismissed in favour of preconceptions, or because of loyalty to other more convenient ways of reconstructing a case to fit in with whatever is more familiar.

Some of what I outline here is repeated in the interviews below (as in Chapter 16) but I am leaving those other accounts unedited to preserve the integrity of each as it had been at the time.

Chapter 13

Response to Stuart Pizer's review[1]

I am here replying to Stuart Pizer's review of my book Learning from our mistakes (2002) in which he suggests that my choice of title for that book had been an act of reparation to my patient Mrs B, as a result of my decision not to hold her hand.

Pizer had convinced himself that I should not have withdrawn the offer of my hand to hold her if things became so painful again. Therefore, he saw my withdrawing of that offer as my 'mistake'.

What Pizer failed to recognize was that I regarded my offer to hold this patient's hand as a necessary 'mistake', to help hold her through the weekend break; but my choice to withdraw from that offer was my choice to stay with what we still needed to work through in the analysis, rather than avoid it. Pizer seemed to have focussed on his own assumptions to the exclusion of what I was trying to convey about the options I had been faced with.

I am indebted to Stuart Pizer for his carefully considered and respectful review of my book *Learning from our mistakes*. In it he raises a number of interesting and challenging questions to which I will attempt to respond.

One problem is that I have always had to limit any presentation of this clinical work to keep within the parameters agreed with my patient, Mrs B, as to how much of it I can publish. That constraint also affects how detailed my responses can be here, because the sequences Stuart Pizer selects to comment on all took place in the context of the previous eighteen months of this analysis, the details of which I need to keep private.

What I can say, however, is that throughout the early stages of this analysis Mrs B knew of only one kind of security: that which she could make for herself. From the time of the initial trauma, reinforced by her mother's collapse during the surgical procedure, Mrs B had developed a dread of depending on anyone other than herself. Safety, for her, seemed to lie in her not needing others and in her being able to control the world around her so that she would never again be caught off-guard or be taken unawares.

Until the time when I chose not to heed Mrs B's signal to me not to continue trying to explore what might have lain before the known traumas, I had remained careful not to challenge her familiar defence of needing to control me in the analysis. However, during the session in which she had signalled me not to continue, I had formed a hunch that there might be some screen memory defence operating, some other alarming experience(s) hidden behind the traumas so often being described to me. It was only very much later, during the end phase of this analysis, that we came to find what had remained frozen in her mind that we did not have any direct knowledge of until her mother provided the missing detail.

When Mrs B was signalling to me not to go on, my choice seemed to be either to continue not challenging her need to control me or to take a risk in standing up to her over this, knowing that my decision to proceed would almost certainly be experienced as poorly timed whenever that challenge might have been.

As it happened, I was unwittingly re-enacting the trauma of 'the surgeon carrying on regardless', for that is how she then experienced me. And after this we had to work through many months of her painful re-experiencing of that trauma. It can of course be argued, from afar, that my timing was really bad, and I can agree that it can be seen so. But I am not sure that I would necessarily have managed this better had I tried to challenge her control of me at any different time, as I was still bound to be experienced as threatening to deprive her of the defensive system she had relied upon for almost all of her life.

Nevertheless, what grew out of this moment of my challenging Mrs B was a chance for her to discover that I could offer her a firmness that just might have the strength she would need to find in some other person, beyond her habitual reliance upon her self-holding for safety. Only then could she begin to negotiate what still lay ahead in her analysis. For, until this time, she had always assumed that she would never find anyone who could be experienced as strong and dependable in the face of her alarm.

When we came to the session in which I had agreed to allow Mrs B to have the possibility of holding my hand, at that time (on the Friday) I felt I was offering the only reasonable response I could, in the circumstances of her extreme anxiety and with the weekend approaching. Most discussants of this sequence have agreed with this. However, when Mrs B delivered her 'hopeful' dream to me, written out on the Sunday, I was struck by the fact that the central figure in this was described as 'motionless'. It seemed to be an unconscious signal to me that, in getting me to agree to the possibility of her holding my hand, she had been able to reduce me once again to someone controlled by her, someone who was not allowed to move and not allowed to have a separate existence beyond her control. This, after all, had been her most trusted way of trying to keep herself safe.

So, I am not sure that I was, at the beginning of the Monday session, the security figure that Stuart Pizer surmises: a security figure that he thinks collapsed when I withdrew the offer of my hand. In that Monday session, however, Mrs B had seen the central figure (of her dream) as already collapsed. This was before I withdrew that offer of my hand, not after.

In the context of her analysis up to this time, I believe that (on the Friday) I had once again become an object that could not threaten her, because of my being again controlled by her. By the same token, I had also been reduced to an object unable to engage with all that we most needed to engage with if we were to make real progress in this analysis: progress towards her becoming able to risk fuller relating and being able to depend on another person to provide for her what she could not provide for herself. And, when progress eventually grew out of the essential working through of this sequence, that is exactly where we got to in this analysis.

For the above reasons I seriously question Pizer's assumption that my decision to retract my offer of the possibility of hand contact had been 'unnecessary for the forward movement of a thoroughgoing analytic process'. I also still believe that I was truly following my patient's cues, for she had already been indicating that she felt she had to take care of me over the weekend, to make sure that I would survive to see her on the Monday.

In terms of my return to the former position of being controlled by her, Mrs B was also seeing me as collapsing. In that state, either of needing her to protect me from that in her which she had always imagined would be too much for anyone, or of being demoted to the state of being controlled by her, I would not be able to provide for her the strength of a surviving object that Winnicott (1969) speaks of in his discussion of 'the use of an object'. Instead, I would have been colluding with Mrs B's longstanding conviction that the most terrible things in her mind had always to be avoided. And as Dr. Heimann had pointed out, I would then have left her with a confirmed sense of needing to rely upon a phobic avoidance as, apparently, the only way to 'deal' with the assumed monsters in her mind.

However, I fully agree with Stuart Pizer about the importance of the 'incisive declaration' of my despair alongside my resolve to go on even when, subsequently, it felt impossible to go on. This really was a key turning point in this analysis. What puzzles me is that Stuart Pizer then questions this for seeming to show a 'one-person' bias. As I understand the projective-identification process here, it was a profoundly two-person experience. Mrs B's own despair, an unnamed dread in her own mind, had to be communicated to me. It also had to become manageable in my mind if it could ever be named and become manageable in hers. I therefore cannot understand how this can be thought of as showing any bias towards a one-person view of this interaction or the understanding that developed out of it.

Now, one of the most challenging points that Stuart Pizer puts to me is related to the matter of timing. How do I account for what seems like a serious contradiction? It is true that I have often declared my dedication to preserving a state of non-certainty while continuing to explore towards better understanding with the patient, except in a crisis (see Casement 2002, Chapters 2 and 3, in the book under review). So how, he asks, could I have acted with such apparent certainty when I withdrew the offer of my hand in the Monday session? Was I perhaps 'looking for a cue to change course' as a result of my consultation with Paula Heimann?

If I was in any sense looking for a cue during that Monday session, I was looking for confirmation that I would *not* need to withdraw my hand then, or perhaps ever. And yet, when I saw evidence of Mrs B's feeling that she needed to protect me over the weekend, and knowing how impossible it had seemed to be, for her to dare to allow me any existence beyond her control of me, I was even more worried when I saw a further indication of this view of me in her seeing the central figure of her dream collapsing in the Monday session.

Here again I believe we are faced with an extraordinary paradox. In offering my hand I could be seen by Mrs B as agreeing that we need not go on with what had become so unbearable in the Friday session (that we could in effect bypass that by her holding my hand if it ever got too painful again). I was therefore actually becoming strangely like the mother who had not been able to face being reminded of her negligence, then fainted. So, in agreeing to help Mrs B to avoid what had become so terrifying, I was being seen as also unable to face it, in other words as collapsing. I would not then be able to help her to face this if I, too, could not bear it.

At the same time, in withdrawing the offer of my hand, in a different way I was *even more* like her mother (superficially) in my hand now not being available to Mrs B (as with her mother), and yet, paradoxically, I was also profoundly unlike her mother *in choosing to be there for the feelings that had been directed so powerfully at the mother whose hand had disappeared*. Only then did we have a chance to go through the intensity of the very feelings that had seemed to have 'killed' her mother when she had fainted, at the time when Mrs B had been hating her mother for not stopping the surgeon. At the same time she had been intensely needing her to make it all right. But the mother had collapsed.

Now, in the transference, Mrs B was hating me for being just like the mother whose hand was no longer available to her. Eventually, however, she came to realize that I was someone who had actually not collapsed. Instead, she was finding me as *someone who had continued to be there for the feelings that her mother had not been there for*. And those feelings had not destroyed me. She then began to find that her most intense feelings were not, after all, unstoppable or apparently lethal.

Mrs B also gradually came to realize that she did not have to spend the rest of her life avoiding her own most intense feelings, or having to protect others from them. They could be expressed and they could be engaged with. And, to her amazement, I could survive them. Security for her could then begin to be found in a relationship with another person. Likewise, security did not always have to be something that she had to create for herself, by avoiding dependency upon others or by always trying to control them so that they could not have any existence beyond that control.

Nevertheless, the question still remains: 'How could I be so certain, I who usually abjured certainty?' I know that I cannot fully explain this, beyond the fact that this was a crisis that needed an adequate response, so there was a strong element of intuition involved in my judgment of that moment. In retrospect, I came to see my choice as having been rather as it might be for a surgeon when faced by a similar dilemma. Should he follow his intuition at a moment of crisis during surgery, from which a patient might die if he gets it wrong, or should he cover his back while continuing to deliberate his options, even though the moment for prompt action might be lost, with the patient possibly dying because of that delay?

Pizer would, I gather, have preferred me to have discussed the options with Mrs B, perhaps exploring with her the possible implications of either course of action, maybe arriving at some agreement with her that we try it without her holding my hand, but with the possibility of that still in place.

I believe that there could have been several problems with that possible way of handling this situation, even though it would surely have felt more comfortable for me as well as for my patient. I think that preserving the possibility of holding my hand would have kept me in the position of being the apparently 'better' mother, with all the patient's most intense feelings about her mother's absence still being kept split away from the analytic relationship and focussed on the fainted mother.

I also think that, if my continued not-holding of Mrs B had been arrived at by consensus, rather than being so clearly my own decision, Mrs B could have regarded this as further evidence that I was being kept as someone still controlled by her. She might also have seen this safer course (for me) as a further indication that I was, as she expected me to be, afraid of how she might feel towards me if I did not agree to her demands. I also do not think that she could have found such a convincing experience of my separate otherness, beyond her customary control of me, if we had proceeded as Pizer would have wished. Likewise, I do not think that she could have so fully focussed on me the intense feelings that she had always focussed on her mother who was not holding her.

As I have indicated in *Learning from our mistakes* (Casement 2002), when Mrs B came for her final session she chose this particular sequence from her long analysis as the most important for her, and she specifically thanked me for finding the courage to go through this without deflecting any of it away from myself— as would have been the case had she still had the possibility of holding my hand.

Further, it had been the richness of her subsequent experience of this analysis that had led her to speak of it to her mother, telling her of the extraordinary discovery that so much progress had grown out of her experience of not *being able* to hold my hand. Through telling her about this Mrs B had come to find the mother she had lost sight of for so long: the mother who had actually helped to save her life by not holding her throughout the excruciatingly painful time of the essential barrier nursing, without which Mrs B could have become infected and died.

It was precisely there, in that prolonged period of not being held—at the time immediately after the burning when she had been eleven months old, that we came to find what had been lying behind the screen memory of the later time of not being held (when her mother had fainted). That later trauma had been so extreme for her as it had connected with the totally unmanageable experience of the barrier nursing. It was only in the light of this new information that Mrs B and I came to understand why her not being able to hold my hand had come to mean so much to her: far more than just the re-enactment of the mother's hand having been lost to her during the surgery. It had been that other, much earlier and much more prolonged not being held that had remained frozen in her mind. And it had only been when she had found a sufficiently firm holding of her in the analysis that she had gradually become able to join up with that earlier, prolonged and most unbearable, time of not being held.

So, is Pizer right in thinking that *Learning from our mistakes* was (perhaps unconsciously) written as an act of 'reparation' to Mrs B? In suggesting this possibility, I think Pizer is looking for evidence that he might be right, after all, in his view of the sequence under discussion and how he thinks I should have handled it. I am sorry to have to disappoint him. Truly, this book was not in any way written as an act of reparation to Mrs B. Rather, this book, as with *On learning from the patient* is, to a large extent, an expression of my gratitude to Mrs B for her unswerving expectation that I should find the courage to be able to go through all that we went through in order to arrive at where eventually she was able to get.

This sequence was not about keeping rules. It was not about keeping myself in my role as analyst through holding her only analytically rather than also physically. It was not about catharsis or about re-traumatizing this patient through re-enactments of the trauma, as some would have it. Instead, it was about that uncanny connection that sometimes occurs between the unconscious of a patient and the unconscious of the analyst, whereby we can unwittingly tune into something deeply buried in a patient's mind as a way of joining up with what has been kept most deeply frozen. If the analyst can remain sufficiently close to the patient's own experience, and in particular her most unbearable feelings, just possibly these can be engaged with and gone through with the analyst. Then, and perhaps only then, can all that had been most feared by the patient be laid to rest: no longer to be feared, no longer to be avoided.

Note

1   Pizer's review of my book *Learning from our mistakes* (Pizer, S.A. 2004) was published in *American Imago* 61(4):543–556. My response was published in the same issue of *Imago*: 557–564. Reprinted by permission of the journal.

Chapter 14

Further reflections

In this chapter I share some thoughts and observations that I have found to be useful, around common technical issues.

Two uses of a spatula[1]

When I had completed my training with the British Association of Psychotherapists, and just begun my analytical training, I was invited by the BAP[2] to take part in an evening set aside for some discussion of different ways of working.[3] I was asked to present for about ten minutes alongside a Kleinian colleague who would be the other presenter.

As I didn't know where I would focus my presentation, I suggested that my colleague speak first; I would write notes while he spoke. I was hoping to get some ideas during his presentation.

It was then my turn to speak and I looked at my notes. I then found I had not written any notes except for one word, '*spatula*'. My mind had clearly gone into free association while listening to my colleague. I had been remembering Winnicott's observation, when seeing infants in consultation, that healthy babies would resist having a spatula put into the mouth, whereas a less vigorous baby might passively allow this without much protest. Whereas, if he placed a spatula in a dish, within sight and reach of an infant, a healthy baby would begin to eye this shiny and interesting new object, salivating with excitement in anticipation of putting it into his/her own mouth. Soon the infant would reach for this, beginning then to play with it and doing so in all manner of different ways, none of them being determined by anything to do with the purpose for which the spatula had been designed.

I then realised that this one word expressed all that I was wanting to convey about different ways of analytic working, my way having been different from what my colleague seemed to be describing in his introduction.

I had become convinced that analysts do not need to 'push' themselves at their patients, either as a transference object or with their interpretations. As with the spatula games that Winnicott allowed infants to discover, analysts could similarly let their patients 'discover' them, and 'play' with them in whatever ways belonged to where the analytic process for them was going. Winnicott (1971) had also spelled out that a capacity for play is really important for being able truly to engage with therapy.

Some thoughts on analytic space[4]

Space in analysis may be thought of as the interpersonal space between the patient and the analyst, which we try as far as possible to keep free from intrusion, interference or influence, whether from outside the analysis or from the analyst. Whatever happens within this space is normally all part of an analysis. The notion of analytic space may therefore help as a context for monitoring what is happening between the analyst and the patient: how this space is being used and by whom. When it is the analyst who 'puts' something into the analytic space, the patient is usually very sensitive to this and to what it may indicate about the analyst, as that may also have implications for the patient. Unconsciously, a patient will always be registering who puts what into this space.

Further, if it is going to be possible for the transference to be analysed, there has to be a sufficient difference between the objective realities in an analysis and whatever is being transferred. And the patient has to be able to distinguish one from the other.

It is also important that the analytic space does not become cluttered with the analyst's subjectivity. For, with too much of the analyst's personality impinging upon the analytic space, there will often be too much background noise for the melody of transference to be truly recognized. And, in my opinion, transference remains the most convincing way of engaging with a patient's past experiences, as these continue to be dynamically present in the analytic relationship as in others.

So, the analytic space needs to be preserved as a space in which a patient can move between different levels of reality within the analysis, including an awareness of the analyst's subjectivity and whatever the patient may make of this, either in phantasy or as a result of projection or transference.

Impaired analytic space

Now, most of us would say that we are already aware of what I have been saying. But that awareness does not always show in how an analyst chooses to work with a patient. It is not only in relation to newly developed theories that the analytic space can come to be distorted. Some applications of long-established theory can also impair that space.

For instance, there are some analysts who see their patients as largely the author of their own misfortune, seeing the patient's view of the external world as if it were mostly, or even entirely, created by the patient's own projections. The cold mother can be seen as reflecting the patient's disowned coldness; the bullying father can be seen as representing the bully in the patient, in projection; and the patient's experience of the analyst can be treated as if this were entirely a creation of the patient's internal world.

This view of the analytic relationship is, of course, very convenient for the analyst. For anything that is proving to be difficult, anything that is going wrong in the analysis, can be regarded in terms of some assumed projection by the patient. The patient can then be seen as the seat of all that is bad, with the analyst seeming to see him/herself as the fount of all that is good. And, when things get really bad in an analysis, the patient can be charged with 'envious attacks' upon the analyst's assumed 'good breast.' I am of course exaggerating to make a point. But I have heard it aptly put that *a psychoanalyst is someone who sits behind a patient pretending not to be God!*

When an analytic relationship develops in this kind of way, it is not surprising that patients complain that they feel blamed by the analyst; that they feel they are seen as bad; that they seem to be seen as full of destructiveness. And when they do not show benefit from this kind of treatment they can be further accused of spoiling the analytic work. Anything that is not working well can be seen as the patient's fault. In these ways, in my opinion, the analytic space is in danger of being so eroded by the analyst's input that there can be little or no room left for genuine analysis. Instead, the patient may be forced into dealing with how he/she is actually being treated by the analyst.

I know that I am here taking examples from some of the caricature analyses that we sometimes hear about, perhaps more often in Britain than in America, but there are some analysts who seem to believe that this is almost how a 'proper' analysis should be conducted. I believe it is frequently the case that these analysts have been put through a similar 'mill' of a quite bullying treatment by their own analyst during training.

I think we all need to be watchful that we don't fall into affecting the analytic space, to the detriment of the analytic work that we are aiming to achieve within it, although we may not go to the extremes just illustrated.

How we assess the outcome of an analysis may be closely related to how we view the issue of analytic space and freedom for the patient within an analysis.

Do we really provide patients the freedom to *be themselves* that analysis, *par excellence*, is in a position to provide? Or does this analytic space become restricted by the analyst's ways of working or the analyst's ambitions for the patient? It does seem that some analysts can become quite pressurizing of a patient, insisting upon a particular understanding, even a particular direction of the analysis, for it to be regarded as making progress. What then of the outcome of such an analysis? How autonomous to the patient are the changes then achieved? Or, to what extent might change in the analysis have been compliant, however subtly.

More about internal supervision

I now want to consider various ways in which we can use our internal supervision, to help us to preserve the analytic space and the analytic process.

I shall be giving examples (below) of how I explore different ways of dealing with familiar situations, hoping that these will encourage others to explore those similar situations they meet in their own work, or in the work of those they supervise; to consider the implications of different ways of dealing with them.

Listening with two hands

One thing that helps me in this is what I call *listening with two hands*. I use this strange notion to invite people to listen for more than a single way of understanding what is going on in a session. On the one hand we might hear something this way; but, on the other hand, we can hear it in a quite different way.

For instance, *on the one hand* we may be getting a sense that a patient might have been subjected to some sexual abuse from, let's say, the father. But, *on the other hand*, it could be that a patient had experienced a *sexualized atmosphere* in the home, which would not necessarily mean that a child had been sexually abused.

A patient may have grown up feeling that her sexuality did not feel safe when father was around, that she could not rely upon a safe boundary being preserved. This too can be traumatising, in making it feel unsafe even to have sexual phantasies in relation to the father, fearing that what could be imagined could also possibly happen. Rather than knowing that it *could not* happen because of having a confidence that the father would never be like that.

Monitoring in the patient's shoes

As I have already indicated, in order to monitor the analytic process I have found it useful to be asking, 'Who is putting what into this space?' Often a patient is responding to something we have introduced into a session that is not truly connected to what they had been bringing to that session.

In passing, I would also like to say a few words about the well-established practice of letting the patient start each session. Bion used to remind us that we do not know the patient of today. We cannot know where the patient has been since last we met, or where the patient might be at the start of a new session. So it makes sense to let the patient begin; and we can only learn about the patient of today *from the patient*.

Unfortunately, this recommendation (to let the patient start each session) can be observed in a too-literal way. There are some analysts who get into a kind of power game with a patient, rather like two people staring each other out to see who is going to blink first, which I do not believe to be either fruitful or enabling of the analytic process. If we remain silent, as a kind of ritual at the beginning of every session, we are putting something disturbing into the analytic space. We are not always being just neutral in our silence.

I still believe that we should let patients start each session, but sometimes a patient *starts with a silence*. And not all communication has to be in words. So, in practice, we do not have to think only in terms of who is going to speak first.

There are occasions when there is important communication also in a silence. I therefore try to see if I can sense *the quality* of a silence, trying to get a feel for when a patient needs me to respond to this, or whether it may be more important for me just to let the patient 'be' in the silence; accepting this and not breaking into it.

Occasionally, after sufficient time, I might say something like: 'I am getting the impression that you are quite anxious at the moment,' or 'I sense that you may be troubled about something.' Often this is enough for a patient to begin speaking. They may feel heard in this, if I have got near enough to what they have been feeling in the silence. Or, they may feel a need to clarify what had been going on in the silence.

Either way, I think that if we get our timing near enough right on this, a patient can sense we *are trying to understand even when they are not speaking.*

On the other hand, when an analyst stays resolutely silent, as if governed by some rule about letting the patient speak first, I do not think that a patient necessarily feels understood in this. More likely a patient will feel manipulated by a prolonged silence, this being prolonged as much by the analyst as by themselves.

Example

I once heard an experienced analyst speaking about a patient who had not spoken for several months. The patient had attended for all sessions and the monthly fees had been paid, but the patient had continued not speaking.

In supervision I tried to explore what the patient might be communicating by not speaking. From this the analyst began to say some of what he felt he could be picking up in those silences; and, after only a few sessions, the patient returned to speaking.

It seemed possible that the patient might have been testing the analyst, to see if he could tune into unspoken communication: that which lay *beyond words*. Only after the analyst had shown a readiness to listen beyond the spoken level of communication did the patient resume speaking.

Who is putting what into the analytic space?

Now, to return again to this monitoring of the analytic space. I think that there are many times that can escape our notice, if we do not monitor for this, when a patient is being affected by something we are introducing into a session that feels to be coming from elsewhere than from the patient.

So, with this question in mind we can more readily become aware of how sensitive patients are to the analyst putting something of his/her own into the analytic space. Unconsciously, patients will always notice when the analyst introduces something that does not recognizably relate to their own thinking, as this may reveal something about their analyst, perhaps indicating something of his/her priorities or concerns, or what the analyst is expecting of the patient.

For example, if we bring in something from a previous session, this may not be where the patient or the analytic process has been going since that last session. So, anything that the analyst introduces into a session is likely to be experienced as an impingement upon the analytic process, to some extent deflecting it and maybe influencing how it then proceeds.

There is, however, one exception to this basic approach to a session, when there is something being avoided from an earlier session. But I think it is always useful to wait until that avoidance is sufficiently evident for the patient to be able to recognize this, as an avoidance, when attention can be drawn to it. There is often something to be understood about an avoidance, for instance in seeing the patient's difficulty in facing whatever is being avoided.

My reason for focussing upon the analytic space is that I believe we can so easily influence the analytic process, at the risk of distorting it.

It was, I believe, with this in mind that Bion used to recommend to analysts that they start every session 'without memory, desire or understanding'. And I don't think that this was meant to be a prescription for elderly analysts, who might in any case be starting to be in that state of mind! Rather, it was in order to preserve the analytic process from distortions that might come from the analyst.

It is all too easy to select, from what a patient is saying, whatever we think we can link with our own thinking about a patient, as when we are looking for transference or expecting to see things in terms of some particular theory.

In selecting as we do, we are telling our patients as much about ourselves, and what *we* consider to be important, as we may be telling them about themselves.

A matter of *shape*: compliance or protest?

A patient once provided me with an image that lends itself well to the issues I now wish to consider, with regard to compliance or protest in an analysis.

This patient said she felt like a round person in a square world. This was said in the context of her working for her doctoral degree with a supervisor who seemed unable to respect the fact that she came to her research from a different position than that of his other students. She came from a particular field of experience which had inspired her to do her chosen research project, but she felt that her supervisor seemed to want her to start from scratch, as it were, as if she were a student straight from college. He also seemed to want her to do *his* research rather than to pursue *her own*.

The effect of this clash had been that the patient felt her PhD supervisor had been wanting to knock her into *his kind of shape* rather than being able to respect the shape she has; to make her 'square' rather than to respect her 'roundness.'

Playing with this image, it occurs to me that we each of us have our own autonomous shape, whatever that might be. I regard the task of psychoanalysis as that of fostering the shape that belongs to the individual, not to change it. I therefore do not think that it is a proper use of analysis if we are, in effect, trying to *impose* something on a patient, let alone trying to impose our *own* 'shape'.

Any one of us might be naturally round or naturally square, or any other shape for that matter. If, let's say, being round is the true shape of a particular individual, then I think that we should be able to celebrate that roundness, or the squareness of another; rather than to treat either as out of line.

Of course, analytically, there must be a place also for being concerned about a narcissistic attachment to one's own shape, if that is based on pathology rather than health. But, I think there is a place for respecting an individual's natural shape when this does not in itself indicate pathology.

What then concerns me here is when someone has had, as it were, their own shape of roundness knocked out of them, so that they can be moulded into being (let's say) square; what then? We can then find ourselves confronted by a convert to that squareness, which is where the trouble for others can begin. For converts, who have given up so much in allowing their own shape to be lost, may then feel driven to deprive others, too, of what is most true for themselves.

For such is the dynamic of conversion. Others have to be persuaded to agree in order that old doubts should not be stirred into questioning a new-found position of certainty.

My reason for describing this in some detail is that this process of giving up something of one's own mind, for the sake of the analytic training, may be more of the analyst's devising than of the patient's, and it is something that can happen in any analysis if the analyst acts too much from a position of authority, tinged as it can be with the sureness (even certainty) of their own training and experience.

Using a patient's words

I think we need to consider, from a patient's point of view, the implications of using or of not using the patient's own words.

For instance, I think we need to be careful that we do not play back to a patient the same strong language *used by* the patient, unless we include what I regard as a 'qualifier', which aims to keep the analytic space open for further enquiry. I'll explain what I mean by a qualifier.

If a patient has been speaking of someone as 'bloody controlling' I would be careful not to be speaking in the same terms about that person. I might instead say something like: 'I see there are times when you feel that person can be very controlling.' I include here the qualifier 'at times', as in saying: 'There are times when . . .'

I am being careful here not to collude with a notion that is said to be timeless, as if the other person in reality is *always* that way. I am also trying to leave room for exploring a difference between how the other person may actually be and how that person is being experienced by the patient.

These are very small differences but in order to keep open a neutral space in which we can look at statements like these, I think it is important to preserve a space in which we can move between how a patient experiences the other person and how that other person might actually be.

There are many other examples that we could all think of where it is useful not to join with a patient's view of other people, as in their use of such words as 'always' and 'never', or to join with their view of the world in terms of *black and white, all or nothing.* Most of life belongs in the grey areas between these extremes.

Incidentally, I also try not to suggest that I 'know exactly' how a patient is feeling. Although I might wish to present myself as empathic, by saying, 'You were probably very upset about this,' the patient may simply respond by saying, 'Yes.' I am then not sure that much is gained by this. Instead, I might say: 'You are not really saying how you felt about this,' leaving room for the patient to join up more fully with his/her own feelings.

Even though it might sound good that I can sense a patient's feelings without being told, I believe that something can be lost when a patient is not given space to identify something of his/her own actual feelings, to find words for them, whatever they might be. And they may not be as I imagine.

Instead, I prefer to make the sort of observation mentioned above ('You are not really saying how you felt . . .') to which a patient can respond in whatever way, rather than to ask a question about how the patient feels, as that puts a pressure on the patient to answer.

Returning to a patient's own words

There are times when we are with a patient who pronounces a word differently from how we do, or who uses a word wrongly. When it is a mispronounced word, it can be difficult to know whether to use their mispronunciation or to sound like a school teacher by correcting them.

An example

I had an interesting example of this with a man who had been turned away by a number of doctors and therapists because they saw him as 'too violent' for them to take into treatment.

This patient had assumed that, for the same reason, I too would not accept him for therapy. But, during the initial consultation, I came to realize that his problem was not that he was *actually violent* but that he was *afraid of his own violence*. That seemed to be why he behaved in ways that made other people afraid of his violence. I sensed that *this* could be his way of (unconsciously) communicating something of his own fear and his need for help with this. Once I had clarified my way of seeing this we were able to enter into some really useful analytic work.

One day this patient was describing his wife's frequent anxieties about her health, she seeming to be quite a serious hypochondriac. The patient then said that whenever she went to the doctor she would not leave until she got a prescription. 'But,' he added, 'the doctors are almost certainly just giving her *place-boes*.'

This patient was an extremely intelligent man, largely self-taught from his extensive reading. I was therefore pretty sure he had only seen the word *placebo* in books, having never heard it spoken. That was probably why he pronounced it as '*place*-bo,' pronouncing it phonetically, as it appears on the printed page.

In my internal supervision, I played with my options. I could use his pronunciation, but he might eventually feel that I had been patronizing him, if he later heard it pronounced correctly. Why had I let him go on mis-pronouncing this? Or I could use my own pronunciation, which he could feel shaming, as if I were laughing at him.

In the end I said to the patient:

> I find it very useful to hear what you are saying here. You may be right about what the doctors give to your wife, but you may also be wondering *what do I give to you*. Do I try to placate you, as in a part of the word you use, which (incidentally) is usually called a '*placeebo*'? Or might I be trying to keep you *in your place*, not allowing you to become more directly violent with me?

From this exploration of his use of this word as '*place*-bo', we were able to get into further analytic work around the issues to do with his violent feelings; how he had usually experienced others as being afraid of him, or as trying to control him; to keep him in his place.

In the examples I am giving here, I am just trying to give a sense of there being different ways of dealing with the situations I describe, learning to consider the implications for the patient in relation to each different way. It is not that I believe that we should always get it right, or even that there is a right way, as if all others would then be wrong. It is in order that we can sharpen our awareness of how we may be influencing the analytic process by what we are putting into the analytic space. I think there is real value in trying to preserve the space from those influences we can so easily slip into the work we do with our patients, often without our being aware that we are affecting the process by how we are being with the patient.

I would now like to give a few other examples that may be useful for us to learn from. Any one of these, or something similar, could happen in our own work or in the work of those we supervise.

How to handle a patient's inappropriate behaviour

A female student had been asked to see a male patient who had been in two or three other attempts at therapy, all of which had ended badly after only a short time. The reasons for that were not known.

The therapist had previously worked in fashion but had chosen to train as a therapist in order to move away from being seen mainly as a sexual object. When she collected a patient from the waiting room, she had led the way upstairs to the consulting room and the patient, following close behind her, had pinched her on the bottom.

As soon as they were both seated the therapist had said to the patient: 'That was completely out of order. I am only prepared to see you if nothing like that ever happens again.'

Now, in terms of establishing the boundaries here, I think the therapist handled this well, particularly as she was still a student. However, if we practise with this for another time, I think there are other ways in which this could be handled.

I think we need to see here that there is more than one issue to be addressed. One is the matter of setting clear boundaries, which the therapist does here. But, another matter, at least as important, is to be able to consider what the patient may be communicating through his behaviour. I think that he may have been showing in action, rather than in words, why he had come to see a therapist, that he had a tendency to relate to women only as sexual objects. He might also be indicating something of why his previous attempts at therapy had failed.

In practising with this I considered the possibility of saying something like:

> I think you know that was quite out of order, but I think we also need to consider what you may be telling me about yourself in behaving in that way.

The difference here is that I am trying to set the therapeutic boundary in more than one way. Not only is it in terms of what is out of order. It is also in establishing myself as therapist. So I would be trying to show the patient that I am there as therapist, to understand his behaviour, not only to forbid it. So from that slightly different beginning, it might be possible to get into the patient's ways of trying to relate to other people: also, maybe, something of why it doesn't work for him. There had been other attempts at therapy which had apparently failed. He might still be in search of someone who could help him to understand his behaviour rather than just criticizing it.

Some further thoughts

There are some analysts who seem not to think in terms of the analytic space. I therefore think we need to wonder how it has come about that those analysts seem to be so removed from any notion of this. For without a freedom to move between the objective realities of the analysis and whatever may be transference, there can be no convincing, or even sane, way in which a patient's part in this can be analysed.

I think the problem started early in the history of psychoanalysis, even with Freud himself. As he began to arrive at an understanding of unconscious processes, Freud was quick to apply what he had begun to understand. Wishing to see his new movement as a science, he sought to demonstrate an assumed universality in his findings. What had been found to be meaningful with one patient would, surely, be applicable to any other apparently similar person.

By such a process as this, that potential spoiler of all analytic experience, *preconception*, came into effect. And with preconception comes a tendency to be less open to different ways of understanding, especially when the clinical process does not fit in with what is being expected. Thus, it will always happen that preconception contaminates the analytic space, in some way, and this can accumulate to the point of making real analysis impossible.

Since Freud, with preconceptions operating, patients began to be merged into types. Procedures were then developed for treating this kind of patient or that kind. The analyst's listening, inevitably, would more readily become tilted towards what was expected, on the basis of theory or of other clinical experience. Inevitably then there comes to be less analytic space within which the inner truth of the individual patient is free to emerge, or at least to be truly engaged with.

Interpretive connections can so easily be made between clinical material and whatever theory is being followed by a particular analyst. And all of this is also likely to be influenced by whatever technique is being promoted by a particular school of analysis. Thus, almost whatever transpires in an analysis can be turned to the cause of demonstrating that this theory or that technique is apparently more effective than others.

So, what if the analyst is getting it wrong?

As I have already indicated, I believe that one really important discipline in analysis is to develop ways in which the analyst can be corrected by the patient, when the analyst is getting things wrong.[5] This is all the more important in view of the fact that the theory and practice of analysis centres so much around the idea that the analyst 'knows' the patient's unconscious, which by definition the patient cannot know. So, the analyst can always claim the higher ground, claiming to know better than the patient. As such, the analyst's assumptions could seem to be beyond correction. My criticism here is less with any particular theory being used than with the ways in which it seems to be used by some analysts.

Some harmful residues from our history

If we read Freud's clinical accounts with an open mind, we cannot help but see occasions when he was seeking to demonstrate or to prove his theories. Then, patients who did not agree with him could always be accused of resistance. He could then seem to justify his pressurizing of a patient in the name of the patient's apparent need to overcome resistance.

In the end, the analyst could always be right; or at least Freud could see himself as being right, whenever he chose. And this has remained a serious hazard in the practice of analysis. Fortunately, I wish to believe, it does not happen so often nowadays. But it is when it does still happen that there is an especial need for there to be ways by which a patient can hope to be better heard.

We still hear of interpretative work, particularly the work of so called 'deep interpretation', being spoken of as 'penetrative'. We also hear of a patient's resistance to such deep interpretation as *a resistance to being penetrated.* If we look at this from another point of view, I think we can also see this resistance as a healthy reluctance to being mentally intruded upon, even raped. So, we need to remain alert to the patient's experience of the analyst, and we need to remember that what we observe in a patient can also be a response engendered by the ways in which we, as analysts, are treating our patients.

Therefore, there may be a lot else that we need to bear in mind with regard to what we observe in our patients. They are, all the time, responding not only to *what* we say but to *how* we are saying it; how we seem to be seeing patients and how we are relating to them. But if we see our task as only that of analysing, without an eye also on the relationship implications of this for the patient, I think that it becomes easy to overlook this perspective. Then, what may in reality be a response to the analyst's ways of working can readily come to be used as apparently proving the interpretive stance being taken.

It is at times like these that I have come to value, in particular, the use of *trial identification with the patient,* reviewing what I have just said, or have it in mind to say, from the patient's point of view: viewing myself sceptically and within the sensitivities of the particular patient. I feel that this view of the analytic interaction can aid us considerably, helping us not to fall quite so readily into the pitfalls of analysis that I have being trying to highlight. Here can be an important way forward, for analysis to become less prone to being dogmatic and self-justifying. And this too I regard as something I have learned through being an independent analyst.

There are, of course, bound to be times when we get things wrong. But, if our style of working is that of being too sure, it can become a real crisis for the patient when the analyst is getting it wrong, whereas if the analyst is more open to correction there is a quite different security available to the patient. It does not have to depend upon a brittle security that threatens to collapse in the face of any mistake, but on something that is more resilient because it comes from the patient finding the analyst being open to correction. And, if we think about it, the too-certain analyst is *also* defending a brittle security, against whatever might threaten it, whether from the patient or colleagues who could be critical.

Some implications for technique

If we bear in mind the fundamental ways in which two people in a relationship interact (as between an infant and the mother; an older child and a parent; a person of any age and another) we cannot afford to overlook the implications of all this for the analytic relationship. We all know that the analyst looks closely at the ways in which the patient perceives and experiences the analyst, in terms of the patient's past experiences and the patient's phantasies. But it is surely just as important that we consider the ways in which the analyst is *being* in the session, in relation to which the patient is also responding, for the patient is often following the analyst just as closely.

It is not enough for an analyst to attribute persecutory anxieties to a patient when the analyst is actually behaving in ways that most people would experience as persecutory. A lot of interpretation *is in itself* persecutory, in the way in which it is given. It is not just that the patient attributes a persecutory quality to what the analyst is saying. A lot of interpretation is also intrusive, is contemptuous of the patient, is controlling, is impinging. There are many characteristics that can be noticed, in relation to the ways in which some analysts interpret, and how they are with their patients. And, even though we may be able to see this more readily in relation to the work of others, we are *all* prone to be like this with our own patients, so we all have to be alert to the risk of that, being careful to monitor our ways of working.

Unless we develop a caution in relation to how we are with our patients we are bound to evoke states of mind, which we will not be able to 'interpret away', even though we can always interpret this away from our own awareness.

How much 'say' does a patient have with an analyst who tends to be too sure?

Sometimes patients are caught into an analysis in which they do not have a sufficient say in what is being assumed about them. They are exposed to frequent interpretations that cannot be challenged. They then have little choice but to leave that analyst or to capitulate. And if they are analysts in training, with the whole training at risk if they leave the analysis, there can be considerable pressures to come round eventually to seeing things the way the analyst sees them. What may result then, I believe, is a collapse of healthy resistance and a resort to pathological compliance. From that may develop a false-self analysis and, eventually, an identification with the aggressor, whereby candidates (later to become analysts) are likely to treat other patients as they themselves had been treated. The resisting stage in this process can then be attributed to some assumed paranoid-schizoid position, and the eventual capitulation can be ascribed to the attainment of a depressive position. Even though this can fit the theory very nicely, it does not have to mean that it is necessarily true. So, how then to unravel this once it has taken a hold? And how to avoid this in the first place?

I regard these as important questions. The answers lie in the areas that I have been outlining above. I think that we can only rescue psychoanalysis from becoming increasingly self-justifying, and circular, through an adequate awareness of what is needed for healthy relating. In no other relationship can it be said that it is healthy to have one person intruding into the mind of another, being so controlling, being so impinging, and even being contemptuous of the patient as some analysts seem to be.

Also, a proper respect for the privacy of a patient's mind is, I believe, too often overlooked. For instance, someone who came to me looking for a training analyst had just come from another consultation about which she said:

> I felt violated by that woman. She seemed to think that she had the right to walk into my mind, without permission or invitation, *and she did not even remove her shoes.*

To understand this one needs to know that the patient came from a Buddhist country where respect for the privacy of the home was always shown by removing one's shoes. I think that this is a most appropriate reminder for us to bear in mind that we should always approach the privacy of a patient's mind with proper respect.

I believe that it is in learning better to recognize the creative endeavours of the patient, often expressed quite unconsciously, that we may enter into ways of relating to the patient that can be both therapeutic in themselves and still compatible with doing proper analysis. With discriminating responsiveness the analyst can learn when to leave alone and when to stand firm, when to allow space and when to confront.

No child can develop securely without being allowed the space that is indicated by a 'period of hesitation', or in the playful use of what is presented (as with the spatula). Also, no child will develop appropriately if a mother fails to recognize the emerging differences between needing and wanting. She should still be willing to meet needs that need to be met, whilst recognizing when to stand firm and to go through the troubles that ensue when a child is not getting his/her own way.

Tantrums can be survived; they do not have to be given in to. Thus a child learns essential lessons for life. He/she will learn from this much more valuably in the context of having a parent who is able to recognize when firmness is needed and when it is her/his continuing availability, for meeting those needs that need to be met, that is still necessary.

Unless we learn to distinguish the different kinds of need that are presented by patients in analysis, and learn to monitor our own contribution to the analytic relationship and its difficulties, analysis will continue to be on the verge of being the cult that it has always been in danger of becoming. I believe that the unaligned analysts in the British Psychoanalytic Society have an important contribution to play here, in helping analysis not to become self-justifying in the kind of circularity that I have been trying to address.

Practising with clinical moments in a session

I often use moments with a supervisee to explore how a particular sequence in a session could have been handled differently. This is not intended as criticism of the therapist. The moment has passed and we have to work with what follows from it. But it may be useful for *other* occasions, when this practising might enable a therapist to consider different possibilities, in how to handle a similar situation when that arises.

This practising is in order to increase the fluency of our listening when we are back with the patient, rather like a musician developing a fluency in his fingers by playing scales. He won't be playing scales when he is in concert, but he can benefit greatly from that practising of scales in preparation for making music.

For instance, a lot of therapists tend to ask questions. I think it is useful to practise with these questions in order to find other ways of dealing with those moments when we might, again, be inclined to ask a question.

What is the problem with questions?

We all have some history in relation to questions, for instance from when we were at school. There we were often told *to keep to the question,* when sitting an examination, not to digress from the set question.

In therapy we can learn so much more from thoughts that come through digressing from a question rather than keeping to it. In fact, in therapy we almost *encourage* patients to digress, to follow where their minds take them. Questions do not so readily encourage that lateral thinking.

For instance, a patient has been describing a situation that sounds to the therapist as quite upsetting, but the patient doesn't give any indication as to what she had been feeling about it. We might wish to show ourselves as being empathic by asking: 'Did you find this upsetting?' But, even if the patient answers 'Yes' we are not really much further on with this.

It would keep things more open for the patient to answer in his/her own way if we were simply to state: 'It is not clear what you felt about this.'

Given a statement like that a patient might say that she felt angry, upset, surprised, ashamed, or whatever. Equally a patient might say that she found it too confusing at the time to know what she felt. The possibilities are multiple here, whereas with a question the response is likely to be more limited. That is why *I prefer to find a statement* I can make, rather than to ask a question like: 'What did you feel?' as some patients may not quite know what they felt at the time.

An example from supervision

A female patient had been speaking to her male therapist about feeling anxious in relation to somebody at work, feeling unsafe with him and afraid that he might exploit her in some way. The therapist, wanting to pick up the possibility of some displaced transference in that description, asked the patient: '*Do you feel like that with me?*'

Almost inevitably, the patient replied: 'Oh, no. I don't feel like that *with you.*'

This is one of those questions which elicits the expected answer. Here the patient is likely to feel a pressure to reply with 'No.' We also need to notice that when a question is put in this way, it can be experienced by the patient as the therapist being defensive, not wanting to be seen in that way.

On the other hand, if the therapist were to say: 'I think you may also be anxious about how safe you are with me,' the patient could hear that the therapist is able to consider that. In other words, the therapist doesn't have to be protected from that possibility. It would be easier then for the patient to say she does sometimes feel unsafe in relation to the therapist too.

Another example from supervision

A therapist had noticed that her patient, who had previously been very prompt in paying her, was now regularly 'forgetting' to bring his cheque book. For several months he had been quite late in paying. When this happened again the therapist had said to him: 'I have noticed that for several months you have been late in paying me. *Is there a problem?*'

I suggested that the therapist might try listening to this from the patient's point of view. She might then see that it could sound disapproving, and it may have been true that she *was* feeling quite irritated with him about these late payments.

Practising with this we might see that a more open way could have been found to approach this, perhaps saying something like: 'I think there may be something here we need to understand,' inviting the patient to explore this.

There could be various meanings in this late paying, not only the possibility of some anger or hostility towards the therapist, which is what she had been feeling in her counter-transference. It could also have been an expression of the patient beginning to move beyond his life-time habit of compliance.

So, the therapist's response here could have been an expression of some *unconscious role-responsiveness* (in her) whereby she may have behaved in a way rather similar to the patient's disapproving parents, in relation to whom he had developed his false-self compliance. Here, in relation to the therapist, the patient may have begun to dare to be more real. But her somewhat disapproving response, 'Is there a problem?' could have set him back into further good behaviour, without finding a sufficiently neutral space in which to explore what his lateness in paying might have been about.

I have only given very ordinary examples here. But, if we keep in mind the value of finding a statement that we can make, rather than a question, we may find there are many occasions when a question is not necessary, when a statement might be more fruitful in allowing the patient to respond in whatever way comes to the patient's mind at the time.

Notes

1 A tongue depressor.
2 British Association of Psychotherapists.
3 See also 'Ways of working' (Chapter 4).
4 Some of this section is from *Learning from our mistakes* (Casement 2002: 100–101).
5 I have listed in 'Ways of working' significant forms of *unconscious criticism*, see above in Chapter Four.

Chapter 15

Kate Schechter interview[1]

Between April and May 2007, Kate Schechter, a member of the editorial board of Beyond the Couch, *conducted an 'interview' via email with me in response to a chapter from* Learning from Life *(Casement 2006), which was published in the same issue.*

Kate Schechter (KS): *Your chapter ends with the comment that much of what you've said about the importance of paying attention to communication in behaviour may be of most value to social workers. Why to social workers in particular? Would you comment on the distinction you are drawing between social work and psychoanalysis?*

Patrick Casement (PC): One of the problems that I have sensed at the interface of social work and psychoanalysis is that, in the social work field, some people are tempted to use inappropriate interpretation. In psychoanalysis, I think there is a tendency to slip into inappropriate action.

In social work, some insight is better used for management. For instance, in the extract from my Chapter 3 (2006) I give an example of this in my work with the client I shall here call Miss X. Instead of interpreting her unconscious belief that her needs would be too much for a single person to bear, hence her spreading of her demands between many different doctors and social workers, I offered myself as the single person upon whom her needs could be focussed. Other people were invited to pass on to me this client's demands, when taken inappropriately to them, so that these would be attended to in my regular visits to Miss X, instead of each demand being treated as if it were a crisis that had to be attended to immediately.

The client gradually became contained in this way. I never interpreted to her my analytic reasons for managing her like this, having other people reporting to me rather than trying to deal with each problem immediately as it was presented. Instead, I shared my reasoning with the team of social workers who had previously been caught into her web of demands.

I believe that it is also easy for social workers to get caught into seeing problems too concretely. It can be quite difficult for some to tune into the internal world of their clients, to see the extent to which clients might experience external reality in terms of their internal world. Internally others may be seen as 'not to be trusted', or 'out to get them', or whatever, all of this based upon the 'objects' in their own minds who had come to be seen in these ways.

Equally, it is tempting for social workers to offer 'solutions' to patients that are too concrete, trying to be a 'better parent' in order to make up for bad experience in the patient's past. What is then so often missed, in this well-intentioned endeavour, is the fact that those intense feelings that belong to the patient's relationship with the 'bad' parent(s) are often kept outside of the consulting room: the 'bad' being still seen as concretely 'out there', and the patient's unconscious contribution to bad experience being overlooked.

By contrast, when a patient's internal 'bad objects' are put onto the analyst, if the analyst can stay with the projections or the transference in this, the patient can have the experience of someone being prepared for, and able to engage with, what may have seemed to be too much for anyone, like a monster in the mind. Only then do these apparent monsters begin to lose their power over the patient. By contrast, just talking about it, with the analyst still being protected from the intensity of what has seemed to be too much for anyone, can keep alive the patient's sense of having to protect anyone who is important to them from that which they still assume will 'destroy' that person.

Another problem with trying to offer a concretely reparative good experience is that patients can see this as indicating the analyst's need to be seen as good and giving, as if the analyst, like others in the patient's past, might need to be protected from the intense feelings patients may have had for those who were previously experienced as failing them.

An analysis of that kind can end with both analyst and patient feeling good about the shared experience, with good feelings for the analyst predominating over bad; and it is sometimes only in a subsequent analysis that it becomes clear to what extent the patient had been protecting the good analyst from all that had been unconsciously feared as a threat to good experience.

A common understanding in analysis is that the 'good analytic object' is that which has survived being used to represent all that had been worst in the patient's past experience. This is a difficult notion, especially for social workers. I think it is only when they have really been through a similar analytic experience that therapists can appreciate the profound truth in this understanding.

KS: So what would you say from your experience of being a social worker has been of particular value to you in analysis?

PC: I particularly came to see the value of recognizing *communication in behaviour*. Communication does not have to be just in words. This applies to adults too, not only to infants or children.

As an example of that, I came to see the invaluable insight in Winnicott's notion of 'the anti-social tendency' whereby he noted that there is often an important communication in early delinquency, or what he called 'pre-delin-quency'. From this I came to recognize what I later called 'unconscious hope', in that people (young and old), especially when disturbed or distressed, often go in search of what is needed, frequently indicating this through behaviour.

I also came to recognize a crucial difference between 'needs' and 'wants'. I came to see needs as needing to be met and wants as sometimes needing to be frustrated. This led me to discern the extreme importance of *setting limits*, illustrated in my first published paper, 'The setting of limits: a belief in growth' (1969). The content of that paper is all in the title. It was based upon Winnicott's observation that one of the most important but difficult responsibilities of a mother is to be able to offer her infant a 'progressive failure to adapt' to demands, introducing the infant to its developing capacity to tolerate degrees of frustration that had not been possible earlier on.

KS: Regarding the supposed utility of frustration, I am most familiar with the movement in self psychology from 'optimal frustration' to 'optimal gratification' to 'optimal responsiveness'. Would you tell me more about how you see the difference between 'needs' and 'wants' and how you came to draw and understand the distinction? How does frustration work?

PC: I give an example in my latest book, of a social work client who had been helped out of a serious debt by a grant that I had raised for her, so that her most urgent debts could be settled and the remaining debts could be paid off by her in weekly amounts that would be manageable.

It had been clear that this client needed the initial help given to her, so that she could manage the debts that remained. However, when she later told me she wanted to spend a further big amount on something she didn't actually need, but very much wanted, I made it clear to her that I would not make that decision for her. Instead, if she went ahead with this, she would have to find ways of paying off the new debt herself. I would not be able to justify asking a charity for another grant to pay off something that we both knew she didn't actually need.

It was this client who threw things at me when I stood firm on this. Later, when she had somehow managed to pay off the additional debt, I gathered she had learned something important from my being firm. I had said 'No' but I had continued to visit her each week. She realized that this was because I had cared enough to take her anger, and to stand firm in my belief that she could find her own way to deal with this. She had likewise found she could say 'No' to her children, when they had been demanding more sweets or presents, etc., which was how she had managed to pay off that new debt rather than spending money on the children in order to feel good through giving, as before. She had also discovered that stronger kind of love for her children, in being able to bear being hated when she knew she was actually trying to be a good parent rather than a spoiling one.

From working with that client demanding money from me, when I had told her I would not be offering her an easy way out of her new debt, I came to realize that a good 'parent' is often tested to see if there is a sufficient love for a child, or caring for a client, to be able to stand being treated as if he/she were a bad parent, especially when faced by a tantrum in a child or manipulative behaviour in an adult.

Even though these demands or requests might often seem to be quite innocent, they can sometimes be an invitation to avoid difficulties in the therapeutic relationship rather than actually attending to what most needs to be attended to. This led me to realize the truth in that saying, about a good analytic object not being that which is better than what had been experienced before, but someone who is able to survive being used to represent the 'bad objects' in the patient's mind.

KS: I note that you always stay extremely close to data, and I am wondering if you also have a story about the progressive quality of the 'progressive failure to adapt' that a mother offers her infant, thereby introducing the baby to his own capacity to tolerate degrees of frustration.

When you are working with an adult, do you see the 'progressive' quality as a cumulative series of developmental steps spread over time? How analogous is this process to development in childhood? Do you also find the concept of regression useful? It strikes me that the time dimension is an especially important part of your theory of practice; and in view of the demand today for brief, medicalized treatments, I think you have some very important things to say about time and temporality in treatment.

PC: I have already given (above) most of an answer to this. In analysis, I came to realize that when a patient is in regression it may be necessary to allow the patient to be in control of the analyst, but only for a while.

With my burned patient, Mrs B (*On learning from the patient 1985/1991;* and *Learning from our mistakes 2002*) I allowed her to control me for most of the opening phase of that analysis until I felt she was needing and might be ready for me to differentiate myself from her view of me as having to be under her control, or apparently having to be protected from all that she had come to assume the 'other' would not be able to bear.

It was when one day I did not stop speaking, when she had (as often before) put up her hand to signal me to stop, that we then began to move into a new relationship in which she could discover that I actually had a strength in myself to survive, not still needing her to protect me from all that she had formerly assumed would be too much for the other person.

KS: You say 'until I felt she was needing, and might be ready for . . .' Could you tell us more about those transition points, the 'until' of the treatment process? How does one know one has arrived at such a moment? I believe that in the old days these were considered junctures, where the 'transference' had become a 'resistance' and needed now to be addressed as such; do you think of this development at all in these terms?

Regarding the value of preserving boundaries, and saying No to demands, I see a man whose life has taken a turn for the busier, from an extreme form of isolation and stagnation. He and I both view this movement from stagnation as a direct exemplification of his growth.

Until recently I have tacitly complied with each of this client's requests for schedule changes, but lately I have noted a different, demanding, somewhat demeaning quality to these requests, and a feeling in myself that some of these are gratuitous and I am in some way being tested. In my view, my patient is showing me his sturdiness and readiness to be confronted more directly with something that has been split off.

My question for you is whether the 'value of preserving boundaries' isn't better put as a 'value of knowing-when-to preserve (versus when to interpret) boundaries'. As I see it, this cannot be a normative matter in a treatment that has momentum. What do you think of this more relativistic view?

PC: I completely agree with this. I don't mean it to be thought of, in standing by boundaries, as something that has to be fixed and rigid. However, I do believe that we need to recognize that issues to do with boundaries are always important. We do therefore need to move from making exceptions to recognizing when exceptions have themselves come to be regarded as the 'norm'.

KS: When exceptions become a problem, then I believe a patient is prompting us to re-think our position on exceptions or flexibility, to see that these may have outlived their therapeutic usefulness. But I don't think in terms of 'problematizing'. I prefer to address the fact that a reliance upon flexibility may itself have become a problem, which could indicate the need for us to firm up on the arrangements so that both analyst and patient can more clearly know where they are in relation to the arrangements, as in the example you refer to.

PC: As I said earlier, with regard to analytic insight, with some clients I came to see the value of 'insight for management' rather than just for interpretation. In analysis, insight may often be of value in helping us to *manage ourselves*, not necessarily for interpretation to the patient. Thus the need for internal supervision, which I learned from students who were internalizing me as supervisor. I had come to see that some students were using me as if I had become an internal SUPER-visor, leading them to feel disabled rather than enabled.

KS: Regarding 'insight for management': when you say it can often be of most value in helping us manage ourselves, I presume you mean that kind of silent process of self-interpretation that you are known for in your work on internal supervision.

How would you compare this to the more traditional idea of 'self-analysis', as an ego function that one takes from one's own experience as an analysand? How conscious and cognitive a process would you say it needs to be? How do you see the learning from one's own analysis and the learning from one's work with clients as related?

PC: I see these two as closely interconnected, but nevertheless somewhat different. Monitoring oneself from the viewpoint of the patient is not necessarily an extension of one's own analysis; but it may well throw up pointers for more self-analysis, as when we may have been stepping back from something difficult; or defensively interpreting something away from ourselves as if it were only transference; or in returning to the patient's history rather than finding a way of staying more clearly with the issue between the patient and oneself in the present; to be *stayed with in the present*.

I think of the process of internal supervision as becoming, with practice, mostly pre-conscious rather than conscious, as when a musician acquires a fluency in the fingers by practising scales. I believe that, with practice, we become more able to be fluent in our thinking in a session; more readily able to sense the implications of what we are hearing, and in what we may have it in mind to say or may already have said to the patient.

KS: In monitoring yourself from the viewpoint of the patient, how do you then work with material that is warded off or defended against?

PC: Another thing I came to recognize from social work, with regard to working with unconscious guilt from a position of seeming to be not understanding why guilt is felt, rather than too readily offering to understand this at the cost of sounding as if we were seeing it as rational, thus *adding to the guilt* rather than helping to ameliorate it.

It is difficult to expand on this without an example. It was when I prematurely interpreted to a client, in social work, that I believed she was attacking herself (in the skin irritation she had developed after her husband had died) because I thought she felt guilty about having so often and openly attacked her husband (in my presence too) before he died of a heart attack.

This client heard what I said as if I were saying she *should* feel guilty. A colleague had commented, in a case discussion, that I had '*merely added insight to injury*' and I think she was right. My comment had been experienced more as an accusation than as an interpretation.

Instead, I might have waited until I could perhaps have drawn the client's attention to what certainly looked like self-attacking, in her constant scratching herself that was drawing blood, as if there were something under the skin she was trying to get rid of, but then wondering with her what this might be about. I now think it is always better to be listening and speaking from a position that is more clearly an 'ego position', seeing a sense of guilt but wondering why it is there, rather than sounding as if we were speaking from a 'superego position', as if we were thinking the patient *should* feel guilty.

KS: *I trust that we will hear more from you on this topic in the near future. Thank you, meanwhile, for this opportunity to speak with you.*

Note

1   Published in *Beyond the Couch*, 2, December, 2007, The Online Journal of the American Association for Psychoanalysis in Clinical Social Work. I am grateful to Kate Schechter for her creation of this email dialogue and for her permission to include it here.

Chapter 16

Thérèse Gaynor interview[1]

This is a transcript from a taped interview (2010).

Thérèse: *First, I want to welcome you back to Ireland, Patrick, and to say how great it is to have this opportunity for a conversation with you. Without any real agenda, maybe I can begin by just asking about the direction your work is taking. I understand you're no longer taking on patients . . .*

Patrick: I stopped seeing patients altogether when I was seventy, five years ago. I gave three years' notice to all my patients because I didn't want to die in harness; and, even more, I didn't want to go on working for years *after I'd died* like some of my colleagues!

Thérèse: *Can you say more about this?*

Patrick: Well, I recently met an ex-supervisee in Waitrose. She was in her late eighties and she couldn't remember who I was, even though she'd been to me for supervision. After I reminded her who I am, and that she did know me, she said: 'Oh yes, of course. I'm glad I've met you as I'm still taking patients, so please refer . . .' I think some people carry on much too long, maybe as an alternative to a pension plan . . .

Thérèse: *So was it always your plan to finish seeing patients when you turned seventy?*

Patrick: Yes, I planned to finish at seventy in order to have the freedom to travel and not being tied to fixed holiday times. My wife had put up with that for forty plus years, and we have grandchildren in Australia; so now we can just jump on a plane and go.

I still do some supervision on the understanding that it's when I am in London and available; and when I'm not, I'm not. It doesn't have the same structure as would be there if I were seeing patients.

Thérèse*: Staying with supervision, what are some of your thoughts around the role of a supervisor?*

Patrick: I think a supervisor has a particular function, in being somebody who hopefully *believes in* their supervisee as a therapist to their patient, rather than behaving as if the therapist were not competent but, with enough nagging, might become competent. That is always more undermining rather than supporting.

There needs to be what I call a *supervisory triad,* a supervisor helping to 'hold' the therapist who is 'holding' the patient. This notion is really a parallel to the notion I attribute to Winnicott (even though I can't actually find it in Winnicott) the *nursing triad.* That is how a mother needs to be supported, by somebody who believes in her as mother, not by somebody who offers themselves as a better mother. Any 'better mother' is always undermining, particularly for a first-time mother.

Thérèse*: I'm curious as to what your response might be, should you find yourself wondering about the competence of a supervisee, or about their competence around a particular aspect of their therapeutic work?*

Patrick: If I hear that something personal might be getting in the way of the clinical work, I would never allow myself to wear the therapist's hat with a supervisee. But I might confront. I might say 'I think there is something personal here and I think you might need to do some homework on it, maybe with your therapist or someone else, but not with me.'

I also ask the question: 'Who is putting what into the analytic space?' and if it is something from the therapist, which does not come in response to something already brought by the patient, then that could be a sign that there's something being brought into the space that doesn't necessarily belong to the patient, and it could be imposed by the therapist. But I know that I am not exactly answering your question about competence.

If a therapist brings in something from outside a current session, this can often hijack the session. The patient may then continue around what the therapist has brought in, but I think it can deflect the analytic process: the process that belongs to the patient, rather than one that is seemingly created by the therapist.

The same is true if therapists bring in something from their own experience. I don't think using one's own experience directly with a patient is advisable. Instead, one can draw on it; one can, for instance, make some general comment such as: 'Sometimes people have experienced (whatever) in a such-and-such a way,' rather than say how I might have experienced it. That, in effect, could be inviting a patient to become curious about the therapist, which I think is usually counter-productive.

With a supervisee, I think the boundary is a bit different. In supervision I do sometimes draw upon my own experience, as I don't see the supervision process as a direct parallel to the therapeutic process. I don't see myself behaving as a model to the supervisee as I might be with a patient. I am not with a patient; I'm with a supervisee. So sometimes I will allow myself to free associate to something the supervisee has brought, in a way I wouldn't with a patient. For instance, when I am supervising somebody I might say: 'The problem with your patient brings to mind something I encountered with a patient of mine . . .' and I give an example which might throw some light on the supervisee's case. So I think, with a supervisee, there is a place for some careful use of one's own experience.

Thérèse: There have been times, as a supervisor, when I find myself offering what I can only really describe as an educative piece to the supervisee, and I'm curious about what you think of the idea of supervision as, in part, an educative space?

Patrick: I think that a lot of my work with supervisees could be regarded as educative in that, a lot of the time, I am practising with clinical moments, as when a clinical moment is being presented and it could have been handled differently.

Now there is no value in saying: 'I think you should have said such and such,' because that moment is gone and it might just make the supervisee feel bad. On the other hand, I could take a moment to say: 'I think it may be useful to practice with this for another time; so, if you respond the way you did here, we could consider how the patient might experience that, perhaps not in the way you intended. But, if we practice here, we might find other ways of handling it.'

For instance, in the area of reassurance, a useful teaching example that I sometimes use is to imagine being with clients or patients who are in black despair, and trying to help them to feel better by saying something like: '*There is light at the end of the tunnel.*' Now, if we listen to that from the patient's point of view, it becomes very clear where the therapist *is* and where the therapist *is not*. The therapist is not in the tunnel, in the blackness with the patient. The therapist is in the light, as if saying: 'It's nice out here, why don't you come and join me?' That is of very little use to a client or patient. It just underlines how distant the therapist is from being alongside the person in the blackness of distress.

Thérèse: I hear something about tolerance and the capacity of a therapist to be with what may feel intolerable for the client, and to journey alongside them through this.

Patrick: This is certainly part of what I am saying, and I'm also trying to consider something that I find to be a useful way of thinking about trauma: as *'that which cannot be borne alone'* because that can help us to find a function alongside the person who is in trauma. If we can make anything different at all it's by being with them, alongside them, as they engage further with their trauma so that they're not now so alone with it.

If a patient is in pain and we're not also in pain, then we are defending ourselves. It's to do with surviving the worst in a patient, but there are two very different ways of surviving it.

One way is leaning back in one's chair and pontificating about what the patient is going through, and we're then light years away from the patient. We're protected from the pain and, of course, we can go on functioning, thinking we're being clever but we're not being useful.

So, when I'm with a patient who is in pain, emotionally if not literally, I see my position as being on the edge of my chair. And when it's the blackest of times, the only thing that has actually helped, with a number of patients I can think of, is when I share my sense that there is nothing that I can do or say to change this. The only thing I can offer is *to be alongside them in this, for however long*. When I've found a moment when I know that's been true and I've said it, it's actually changed things for a patient.

I also want to say a word or two about tears. I mention this in my last book, *Learning from life* (2006, in the chapter on 'Mourning and failure to mourn') when I was with somebody who had lost a baby as a result of having a test to see if the baby was alright, a test because of her age. The test was fine but the baby died because of it. She was in the most acute and relentless pain, and she needed to just pour out her pain in unbearable crying. She couldn't use the couch. She needed to be on a chair. And I was sitting on the edge of my chair just looking into her face, being with her; not able to say anything meaningful, just sometimes making a kind of *I'm still with you* sort of noise.

In the third of these sessions it was so painful, I realized that tears were forming in my eyes. But I believe that we need to be able to contain our own difficult feelings during a session so that these do not intrude upon a patient. The place to process that is outside the session. We therefore need to contain our feelings as well as we can during a session.

So I tried not to draw attention to the tears forming in my eyes, as by wiping a tear away, because I didn't want to deflect from the patient's pain by bringing attention to my own tears. I just let happen what was happening, and at the end I said to her what I've already indicated: '*I know there's nothing I can say that could change any of this, or make any of it feel any better, but I can still offer to be with you in this.*' And she said: '*You don't need to say anything, your face has said it all.*'

I think it's not inappropriate for a patient to be aware of the fact that we are sometimes in difficulties alongside their difficulties, but they need to have a sense that we are able to bear it. If we indicate anything that could be read as our not being able to bear it, then they could feel somehow that their distress might be too much even for the therapist. So it's a difficult balance.

If we are engaging with something that is extremely difficult for a patient, I'd expect it to be difficult for me. And I know that if it's not being difficult for me, then I have to ask myself, why am I keeping myself at a distance from this?

Thérèse: That's clear, so I guess a balance can be drawn from our experience and our ability to attune to the quality of the resonance; holding and responding appropriately.

Patrick: I can give a brief example of somebody who had been very seriously traumatized and abandoned by what happened in his childhood when he was two. He was very much locked into his head. He had never cried in any session.

The childhood problems were talked about but never re-experienced, as far as I could tell. We then came to the third long summer break and I made some cliché-sounding comment about it being difficult that I was going away just then. He responded with absolute scorn, saying: '*Well, of course, all analysts are saying that kind of thing in July.*' I felt quite properly jogged into re-thinking.

After a long pause I said to the patient: 'I'm glad you challenged me because it's helped me to realize that, if I listen to this from the point of view of the two-year-old in you, I think the two-year-old could feel that if I really understood what my going away could mean to that child, I would not be able to go away.' And, for the first time, he cried.

Now, I wasn't offering not to go away. I was trying to get across some sense of being in touch with the quality of this absence for the two-year-old; and, at that moment, he felt that I had.

Thérèse: *As you're talking, at different times I can see tears form in your eyes and I can clearly hear the emotion in your voice . . .*

Patrick: Well there are several reasons for that. One, as I said earlier, is that the place for processing the most difficult clinical experiences is not in the consulting room with a patient, but afterwards. I now find that when I'm talking about these things I'm still processing what I was having to contain at the time. So that's the first thing. Another is that I don't think it's always to do with *painful* things that I might find tears in my eyes. Actually, one of the things that moves me most is the relief of finding that something has become possible that might never have been possible. So it's like tears of joy.

I can also think of another kind of tears, which we sometimes meet in a patient and don't always understand, that I have described in my last book. It is from the time when I first came across what I now call *the pain of contrast*.

In what had seemed to be a perfectly normal session, my patient suddenly started crying, and very deeply crying, and I couldn't think what had brought this about.

It took a long time before the patient could say anything. When she could speak she just said: 'It's your voice.' I thought how strange is my voice that it makes her cry like this? After more crying the patient eventually managed to say: 'Your voice is kind.'

She had bumped into a realization that she couldn't recall a single time in her childhood when either her mother or father had ever spoken to her with kindness. So she didn't know what it was like. And then, suddenly experiencing it for a first time, she was flooded with an awareness of what she'd missed that she'd never had.

Thérèse: I'm reminded of what is often referred to as a missing experience and the joy and pain that can be felt in the experiencing of something, perhaps for the first time.

If it's okay I'd like to change tack a little and ask you something about your own journey and the move from psychotherapy to psychoanalysis. I know that my approach to this work reflects something of my own process, my journey and my way of being in the world. I'm curious about the move you made and how you might describe the qualitative difference between therapy and analysis for you.

Patrick: I find it very difficult to be meaningful in describing the difference because I don't think it's just a matter of frequency. I think that with the analytic training, where there is an insistence upon the frequency of sessions, we have an opportunity to discover the potential of psychoanalysis in its truest/fullest sense. But I don't think that it's only with frequency that that's possible.

I think that, if one has had the experience of being able to recognize what's around at depth, and working at depth, we can do that sort of work with somebody who is not coming as frequently; and I've done some seriously important depth work with patients who have only come once a week. But I don't think I would have been able to do that if I had only ever worked infrequently. It's drawing on my experience of analysis that has enabled me to work at depth, also with people who could come only once or twice a week.

Thérèse: Maybe it's not so much about difference; maybe it's more about the quality of, and our capacity for, being with our clients.

Patrick: Well I also want to keep alive an awareness that a good analysis does not end when the patient stops going to the analyst. I think a good analysis is when the analytic process has been sufficiently established for that process to continue way beyond the end of the formal analysis. So I think that, if we can get into that inner process, keeping it alive and drawing on it, we may find that we get far beyond where we had got to in our own analysis. It's not limited by what we actually achieved with our own analyst.

John Klauber used to say: 'It takes at least ten years for an analyst to become an analyst after they have finished training.' And my version of that is: 'It takes some people at least ten years to recover from their training.'

For instance, a well-established analyst in Europe sometimes comes to me for consultation; and on one occasion he was speaking about a patient who had come for analysis four times a week throughout his third year of analysis, but for the last six months had not spoken a word.

I got the feeling that this analyst felt somehow obliged to wait for the patient to speak first, as learned in his training. So I put it to him that, even though I believe in letting patients begin the session, in whatever way they begin, sometimes they start with silence. But there can be important communication in silence. So, if we sense some of that non-verbal communication, I think it's OK to have a shot at indicating something of what we feel we're picking up. At least then the patient has a sense of being with someone who is prepared to work beyond words, rather than only with words.

Once I got this across to the analyst, who surprisingly seemed not to have recognized this for himself, within just a few days the patient was talking again. So in that sense, this analyst may have been someone who'd not quite 'recovered from his training'.

Thérèse: I'm reminded of my own analysis and the part silence played in that, remembering the times when my analyst would offer something and I sensed when this was spot on, or when it felt that it was more about her anxiety or intolerance to remain with me in the communication of the silence.

Patrick: I once had a patient who said to me that sometimes she felt I tried too hard to understand. She then came for a session that was spent totally in silence. I felt I should respect that and not risk spoiling it by speaking. I simply said at the end of the session that what had helped me to remain silent with her was what she'd said previously about me 'trying too hard to understand.'

The next day this patient came for another session which was again fifty minutes of total silence. I didn't need to explain where I was. The day after that she told me she was profoundly grateful because she felt that I had allowed her the first experience she could remember of actually *being free to be herself*, rather than always trying to fit in with the other person. So she felt she'd had a real experience of *being* rather than just trying to please. I think that only worked because it was based on an understanding that came from the patient, which allowed me to listen to the silence in that way, rather than thinking it might be a good thing to remain silent.

Thérèse: Earlier, you spoke about 're-experiencing' and I felt a response that I recognize is attached to the idea of re-experiencing trauma in therapy and how this can sometimes translate into a client feeling re-traumatized. It seems to me that we have a responsibility to our clients to understand the complexity of this re-experiencing something in the present that may have its origins in the past.

Patrick: I'm using the word 're-experiencing' because of an ambiguous meaning in that word. Winnicott in his wonderful, and very brief, paper called 'Fear of breakdown' (1974) talks about people who have experienced trauma at such an early age that the mind could not engage with it and survive. The infant mind had detached itself from the experience as if it hadn't happened. So in one sense it's happened; but, in another, the mind has not engaged with the experience of it. And the unconscious hope seems to be that a time may come when there is better holding around, and the mind is more mature, when it might just become possible (with help) to unfreeze the experience and to engage with it in a way that feels almost like for the first time; a first time of fully experiencing it.

Now, with my burned patient (Mrs B) a lot of people felt that I should have limited her to *talking about* the early trauma whereas she actually got into *re-experiencing* it.

This is what Winnicott means about the important and complex idea of the *survival of the object*. The object is destroyed in the mind, but in reality it is found to have survived being 'destroyed'. So, in her mind, she was 'killing' me and yet she came across the reality that I hadn't been destroyed by it. This transformed her lifelong dread of her own neediness and dependence, of her anger and intense feelings.

All of that became possible for her to engage with, for me to be alive with, rather than feeling that she had to be forever protecting the other person from all of that, as she had always felt she'd had to. Now if I had done the *corrective emotional experience* thing, by offering to be the better mother who was continuing to hold her hand, we would never have got into any of that, and it would not have helped her.

Thérèse: Thus staying in the gap, and creating the containment and safety necessary for what could be described as a negative transference to unfold.

In your work Patrick, I'm wondering where in analysis you feel there is the space for the physical imprints, the sensate memories or the echoes that are so implicit in both traumatic wounding and developmental wounding.

Patrick: Interestingly, some psychologists have been very critical of my work with that burned patient on the basis that, at the time of the burning (when she was eleven months old) they claim the patient's mind had not developed enough of a capacity for memory to be able to recall the experience.

But I'm absolutely certain that there is something else, which I call *body memory*. Because this burned baby had the pain of having been burned, feeling it today and the next day, and the next day after that, and the week after and the month after that, and so on: that would have been imprinted deeply into her mind. She didn't need somebody to remember it for her; her body was remembering it for her until she was old enough to draw on her own re-collected memory of that: remembering her own remembering.

Now what was so interesting, which I go into in my third book (*Learning from our mistakes 2002*) when I revisited my work with that burned patient, was the discovery of something, which neither of us knew about at the time, that lay behind that focus on the moment when the mother had fainted (when the patient had been seventeen months).

All the time, during that part of the analysis, it had seemed as if the remembered trauma had been entirely of *that moment of not being held* that she had consciously been raging about. But when the patient realized she had really recovered from that trauma, and had become alive in herself, she wanted to re-negotiate her relationship with her mother to celebrate her recovery.

The mother (until then) had never recovered from this, still blaming herself, for having exposed her child to the risk of being burned. So the patient described her analytic experience to her mother, telling her that the most amazing thing of all (which had also helped her most) was that her analyst had found the courage to go through the surgical experience with her *without holding her hand*; so all the rage was there for somebody not holding her.

The patient had then described to her mother that long period of the analysis. During so much of that (though she did not know it then) I had been struggling with myself, thinking am I causing her more pain than I should, more pain than she can bear? Maybe I've made a terrible mistake, maybe I should bring it to a halt. But something made me not do that. Many times I had struggled with myself over it.

The mother had then said to my patient: 'But there was *another not holding* that you don't know about.'

This had happened in wartime Europe and there was no hospital able to offer sufficient sterility for a baby that badly burned. Also there were no antibiotics then, or pain relief for a baby of that age. The doctor had therefore said to the mother:

> The only chance of saving your baby's life is if you (the mother) barrier nurse her, which means using sterile gloves, sterile instruments, and you must only handle her in a totally sterile environment. Also, the one thing you must never do is to give into your instinct to pick up your crying baby, to make her better, because that would infect her and she would almost inevitably die.

So, without knowing it at the time, what had been in the room between my patient and me was that endless experience of not being held, alongside a mother-person desperately *wanting to hold her to make her feel better*.

Something had held me back from doing that, and it was such a vivid example of what Freud called *screen memory*. We had been working on the *not being held*, at the only level her mind could engage with, in the room between us. But there had also been this other *timeless experience of not being held*, plus the tension between her being in such distress and me as a mother-person struggling not to disturb her healing.

If I had given into this impulse to hold her, to relieve my patient of her most immediate pain, it would have simply confirmed forever her belief that, sooner or later, her distress would be too much for the other person. She might have reverted forever to the habit of self-holding, and her feeling that she always had to be protecting the other person from her most intense neediness.

Thérèse: What was it like for you, when you heard about this missing piece of history, because as therapists we don't often get to hear what may only come to light post-therapy.

Patrick: It was utterly amazing. It was such an affirmation of everything we had been through. Both the patient and I suddenly knew *that* was what had been in the room between us all the time; even though we couldn't then actually name it.

Thérèse: This seems to me to be a wonderful example of the not-knowing, when we trust what may be a felt sense of what we do not know!

Patrick: Quite extraordinary and such a relief; again the tears of relief. It was such an extraordinary experience.

Thérèse: Your passion is clear and I'm wondering – have you always felt this? Have you always felt the passion and compassion within you that feels so real and alive even in this moment?

Patrick: I know where some of it comes from because, although I don't spell it out fully in my last book, I do touch on this in the first chapter. I was a child who had frozen my feelings of attachment. I then couldn't think why children were crying at my boarding school. What were they crying about? Missing home? But what was there to miss?

I had somehow insulated myself from any attachment. It was only much later that, with the help of my analyst, I discovered why I had once collapsed into the most profoundly deep crying. I won't go into this here but I describe that in the first chapter of *Learning from life.*

So of course I had, and still have, a passion for my work. I think I was very fortunate in being with the analyst I was eventually with, because he was not a man of many words, and a lot of the communication was beyond words.

I have since found myself working far more intuitively with patients than I otherwise might have done, then not relying very much, if at all, on the models that had been around that we can imitate – the way to interpret – the good interpretation, all those things. I much preferred to struggle to find words, however inarticulate they might be at the time, struggling to engage with something, trying to understand it with a patient, and trying to find words for it. I think a lot of patients feel there is something more genuine in that struggle, rather than being with somebody who seems to say: 'Of course, what's happening here is . . .' and out comes another cliché.

Thérèse: It's good to hear you speak about working more intuitively, and I guess for me a great deal of what I believe engages the unconscious is beyond words, as in using integrative bodywork and the choreography of movement. The emerging experience for a client is supported, processed and integrated in the physical, emotional and cognitive realms and there is a sense of moving through or sequencing through, layer after layer.

Patrick: I have great respect for that bodywork. I don't have that skill but I can see the value in it. We get to where we need to get to with patients by different routes, along whatever is most true for you with a patient or whatever is most true for me with a patient. I think it's being true for both patient and therapist that is more important than having the idea that there is one model that is better than another.

Thérèse: I value the integrity of your response and feel how respectful that is. You've written about your experience with, I think, your first therapist and how in that therapeutic relationship you felt blocked (my words) in getting to experience your own feelings of anger because your therapist herself had unresolved issues (again, my words) with anger.

Patrick: I could never be angry with her. She needed, for her own reasons, to be appreciated, needed to be thought well of so that *her* need was blocking off whatever, in me, needed to come into the work with her. And I went to her as a failed suicide.

If somebody is so angry that they try to kill themselves, there is always anger around, and why has it been turned against the self, and why could nobody engage with it? I found myself with a therapist who, for seven years, clearly couldn't engage with my anger. This just confirmed my worst fears of what anger could do. I had to find somebody who wasn't going to be afraid of whatever it was in me that I had come to imagine no one could bear to be really in touch with.

Because of my time with that therapist, my first patients were all seeming to get better; but all seemed to be getting better to please me, thinking I was a nice person and being so helpful, and all that sort of stuff. But there wasn't room, with me as I was then, for them to bring what might be described as a negative transference, to use me to represent the worst in themselves, rather than have me as somebody who seemed to be better than those others by whom they felt they had been most let down.

I'm not now seeing patients but there are two exceptions. I see just two people that I do not regard as patients, who come to see me occasionally for consultation.

The first person, who was in his late seventies when he came to me, had a history of seeing therapists or analysts for almost all of his life, which hadn't done much good and yet he wanted to have another go at it. However, I felt it might be the worst thing I could do to refer him to another one of those people, because they might take him into yet more analysis or therapy. I'd already made it clear that I wasn't taking patients, so what could we do? I said:

I'm not going to think of you as a patient. You've had enough analysis. Instead, I think you now need to discover that you can get along *without* seeing a therapist or an analyst. So, if you like, you can come to see me from time to time to tell me how you're getting on without one of those.

He did that and he was getting on much better.

There's one other person I see on a similar basis, and I think of myself as supervising these two people in relation to their own analysis, rather than have me doing it.

Thérèse: And finally, your books, workshops, seminars etc. have the potential to influence and impact on the lives of many others, most of whom you may never actually meet and I'm curious about how you keep it real for yourself?

Patrick: So, how do I stay real, having discovered that it's possible to be real? Well I would rather die than lose that realness, and I think it may have influenced me away from taking my work to clinical seminars, I feared there might be too much interference, in my clinical work, from people who work differently.

Yes, I could always learn from other people's ways of working, but I have become very protective of a way of working *with* patients: *learning from patients.* That has taught me almost everything I know about clinical technique, and I just didn't want to have that process interfered with by too much preconception coming at me from other people.

One thing I also try to remember to say at any teaching day, because I know that I can sometimes have more influence on others than I intend, is this:

> Please don't do anything differently next week just because of what you've heard from me. That would not be using your own thinking. It would be using somebody else's thinking. If, however, you do find something from me that seems to be of value, you'll come across it again later: when you've had time to digest it.

Thérèse: Thanks Patrick, it's been lovely having this time and opportunity to speak with you.

Patrick: Okay and thank you too.

I also wish to say that I really like your journal's title: *Inside Out.* One of the things I've most been able to celebrate, in my years of clinical work, is being able to let out what had before been locked in.

Note

1   Published in *Inside Out Journal*, IAHIP (Irish Association of Humanistic and Integrative Psychotherapy), Issue 51, Spring, 2007. I am grateful to Thérèse Gaynor for her permission to re-publish this here.

Chapter 17

Questionnaire interview (2016)

Conducted with Shelley Holland of the Brighton Therapy Partnership, this interview was in preparation for the day conference "Perspectives on Interpretation", 19th November 2016.

Shelley: How did you start out in counselling and psychotherapy?

Patrick: I started as a patient in need; a failed suicide. I didn't actually choose to become a therapist. The idea had never occurred to me while I was working as a social worker. In the end I trained mainly to please my therapist, something she saw as better than killing myself! But the training became a false-self solution to my much more fundamental problems. I describe in my book *Learning from life* (2006) how I eventually became a psychoanalyst.

Shelley: Your book On learning from the patient *has been recommended reading on training courses for counsellors and psychotherapists for decades (my own included!). What was the inspiration for this book?*

Patrick: I had not intended to write a book. The idea of *learning from the patient* gripped me when I came to realize that it described an approach to patients that had naturally evolved from my resistance to the more usual application of theory to patients. I felt that I should try to communicate this view of clinical work to others, and my first book grew out of that exploration. It then just took off and it has so far picked up twenty-one translations in the thirty-one years since it was first published.

Shelley: You've now written five books, including an autobiography called Growing up? A journey with laughter *published in 2015. Which of your writings are you most pleased with or proud of? I wondered if you had a favourite, or one that was particularly satisfying to write?*

Patrick: I am naturally proud of my first book as it continues to be much used, now into its fourth decade. But, for me, it is *Learning from life* that I regard as the most important (to me) as it brings everything together: all that grew out of the rather strange journey which led me eventually into clinical practice. The book I most enjoyed writing is *Growing up? A journey with laughter*. It was such fun to write and it was put together to celebrate my return to life, having not been expected to survive my then thought-to-be terminal cancer.

Shelley: There's been a real growth in the provision of counselling and psychotherapy training in recent years. Does this seem like a good thing to you? I wonder if you would recommend a career in psychotherapy to people thinking about training?

Patrick: I have some problems with this. I think that there are too many people wanting to practice as therapists or counsellors, and I think they are a pretty mixed bunch. I also think there needs to be a fuller sense of vocation, preferably growing out of a recognized need for therapeutic help for oneself, rather than it being seen as a job that one might do.

Shelley: You're now retired from clinical practice. What are you enjoying most about being a retired psychotherapist?

Patrick: Although I have been retired from clinical work for over ten years, I still love doing some supervision or consultation. I also appreciate the freedom now to travel when the whim takes, rather than being tied to the working schedule I always offered to patients. Also, it is only now that I am retired that I realize quite what a weight of responsibility, for the lives of others, I had been carrying for the past many years. I don't miss that.

Shelley: If you hadn't been a therapist, what would you have been and why?

Patrick: I don't think I can imagine what else I might have done. I had to follow where my own evolution took me. I just could not have done otherwise if I were still to remain true to myself.

Chapter 18

My time with cancer

An extraordinary journey[1]

Preamble

Ever since I came out of hospital (in 2012) I have several times been asked if I would be writing up my experience of cancer. Until now I have always said that I would not do that, for several reasons. Although I have no problem in talking about my experience, my reluctance had mainly been because I did not want to alarm people. Not all cancer patients go through what I went through.

Another reason for my hesitating to write it up was because I have ended up where not all patients are privileged to arrive. A strange thing about my cancer, Burkitt's lymphoma, is that it usually does not come back once it has been completely cleared. How lucky I am that my consultant can tell me that I am now unlikely to see my cancer again. I wish the same good fortune could be shared by all cancer patients. Nevertheless, it may be that other people can gain something from hearing that a very serious cancer can be survived; can even be beaten. And the treatment of cancer is getting better every year. So I have, after all, decided to write about my rather extraordinary journey.

Finding that I had cancer

We were due to leave for New Zealand on 10th December 2011, but I had been having slight discomfort in my stomach, for a month or so before. My GP at the time had examined me and had decreed that this was a flare up of my existing *hiatus hernia*. A few weeks later he said it might be gastritis. Being concerned not to risk spoiling our trip to New Zealand, followed by four weeks with our daughter and grandchildren in Sydney, I decided to cut out any foods or liquids that might exacerbate my gastric condition. I therefore decided not to have any wine at all.

After about seven days, I declared proudly to my wife, Margaret, that she should also try to go without wine. I had lost ten pounds in seven days. Fantastic. But she didn't think it was quite as fantastic as I did. No one should lose that amount of weight in such a short time. She wanted our GP to investigate, to rule out the possibility of cancer. As we had only ten days to go before leaving for

New Zealand, the GP was able to arrange for me to have an endoscopy and a colonoscopy within the next few days. On the following Tuesday I saw a new GP to discuss the results from those recent tests and we were told that there was 'something there.' It was therefore arranged for me to come in the next day for a blood test.

When I woke on the Wednesday morning I was suddenly feeling more ill than I could ever remember having felt before. I told Margaret that we should not wait until my appointment for the blood test. I felt that I had to get within immediate reach of a doctor, even though I didn't have an appointment. We therefore went in to the morning surgery, saying that I was willing to wait for any doctor who was able to see me. I was prepared to wait all day, if necessary. The new GP (from the previous evening), who happened to be on duty that morning, took one look at me across the waiting room and insisted that he see me straight away. I have no idea what he noticed, but he discovered that my pulse was running at 220. Not good.

I was immediately transferred, in a wheelchair, to an ambulance that had been called. Within minutes, I was taken to the direct admission suite of the Royal Free Hospital (RFH), where a crisis team was already waiting to deal with me. Then, for some seven hours those doctors worked on me to bring my pulse down to a safer rate. They even tried using pressure points, and whatever else, but not before they had tried the more usual treatment of digitalis, or whatever. I heard them prescribe the usual dose, followed by a double dose, and then I heard them say: 'We've never tried this before, but I think we should try doubling again.' Eventually, I was taken up to the heart unit on floor 10 of the RFH, where I was linked up to all manner of monitors, with something like fourteen wires attached to me.

I remember that I was sweating a lot. Also, for some reason, I was left in my day clothes, for quite some time. I can now only assume that this may have been in order not to put me through needless stress in getting me into a hospital gown. It seemed like several days before I was washed. Eventually, being embarrassed by how much I then smelled, I apologized for this to a junior doctor. But he kindly replied: 'You don't smell bad. You smell quite nice.'

I think it was on the second day that I met my consultant, Dr K.[2] She was very straight with us, and it soon became clear that, after I had been through various scans, I not only had a lymphoma but I also had a number of significant blood clots in my lungs. These would have to be treated alongside my cancer, but the treatment was going to be very complicated and I would have to remain in hospital for some time. The initial chemo I began to receive had been a preliminary treatment, this being administered through a mechanically-controlled pump, monitored by a lovely Portuguese nurse called Manuel. He was very attentive, and he knew to act immediately when I reported to him, half way through the chemo being pumped into me, that I was becoming extremely dizzy. He said that my body was clearly not able to take this chemo and he stopped it straight away.

We learned the next day that there was by then a more accurate diagnosis. I had Burkitt's lymphoma. This was far advanced, stage four, and we were told that it was also very aggressive. However, Dr K explained that this was not necessarily a bad thing. As the cancer would be growing very rapidly it would also be more vulnerable to the treatment, but they would have to use their most aggressive chemo in order to take it on.

On my second day in hospital we discovered that the lymphoma had closed off my stomach. This meant that I could not be given any food by mouth. For the first month I received only a saline drip; I never understood why I could not be given anything more nutritious than that until the second month, but throughout I totally trusted the team's judgment. In all I lost something like 56 pounds in 56 days. A fantastic diet for losing weight, but not to be recommended. I became Belsen-like in my thinness, my legs just bones. But the interesting thing about it was that I never once felt hungry.

Mostly, I was very well nursed. And sometimes I was lucky enough to be looked after by those who were truly dedicated to nursing. It was easy to tell that, and I would then always tell them: 'You are a really good nurse.' I wanted them to know that.

However, there was one nurse who seemed to have no sensitivity at all. On one of my first nights in the heart unit I was not getting to sleep. I wanted to ask for another sleeping pill but didn't want to buzz the nurse. Perhaps I could ask when he next came in to see me, which was usually every hour or two. When he eventually came it was about one o'clock in the morning. I was then firmly told 'no sleeping pills could be given after midnight.' How absurd, I thought, as I was hardly going to be driving a car the next day. But, 'No.' So, I was left to get to sleep, or not, for the rest of the night.

Then at about three o'clock, when I had just dozed off, this night nurse came back to see me. He had a tube in one hand and said that he was going to have to insert this into my nose, as my stomach had to be drained of any liquid that might collect there, now that my stomach had been closed off. I asked why it had to be done there and then, as I had only just got to sleep. He said that in the notes it stated that this tube should be inserted 'as soon as possible'. But could it not have been left until the morning? No, it had to be done there and then. So, this nurse shoved the tube down my nose, and did this so roughly that my throat subsequently became ulcerated, which continued to trouble me for all of the two months that the tube had to be in my nose.

After a week or so in the heart unit, I forget exactly how long, I was transferred to the lymphoma unit where I was put into a single room. I then remained in isolation throughout, to preserve sufficient sterility while my immunity remained low or zero. At such times, any visitors who came to see me had to be equipped with sterile gloves and an apron; and mostly they kept to a safe distance from me. We got quite used to this.

In preparation for my main chemo treatment, which I was told would be four courses altogether, I had to be given a special line which was inserted into a vein.

This line was multiple and was to be used for giving me the chemo, but also (I think) for giving me saline and for taking bloods as often as necessary. That procedure initially went well. But when I was about to start the first really aggressive chemo treatment, a duty doctor came to see me before leaving the hospital for the weekend. It was six o'clock in the evening. When this doctor looked at the line, which had been inserted to a point very near my heart, she noticed that it was forming clots. 'That line must come out immediately'.

The junior doctor who came to remove the line then told me he was very impressed that a doctor about to go off duty had recognized the problem. He said: 'That was a very good spot.' But the next problem was to find another suitable line (multiple) and to find someone suitably trained to insert it.

In the meantime, Bishop Peter Wheatley (then Bishop of Edmonton) came to see me to give me what I thought of as the 'almost' Last Rites. Actually, it was the 'unction of healing'. I told him of the line problem and that they might not be able to get my chemo started until Monday, giving the cancer free rein for another several days. He said: 'We'll just have to pray.' Almost immediately after he'd said that, someone came into my room to tell me that they had unexpectedly found someone still in the hospital (being then late on a Friday) who would be able to insert the line. So, all was well. I said to the bishop, 'That was the quickest answer to prayer I've ever come across.'

When I started that chemo, the first full chemo, I didn't know what to expect. It was very strange. I found myself sinking into a state of such low energy that every movement seemed to require of me more energy than I felt able to summon up. That deep lethargy was absolutely the worst thing about the treatment. Fortunately, however, I never once had the experience of nausea that one so often hears mentioned in relation to chemotherapy. The doctors and nurses were marvellous. They kept me completely protected from nausea throughout my entire time in hospital, my five months there. I wish that all chemo patients could be similarly protected from nausea. Also, I was never once in pain.

After some days I was given a shower, sitting in a chair. This was my first full wash since being admitted. It was glorious. But the next time I was showered I was left sitting naked on the chair, forgotten, only partly dried, and I became progressively cold. Eventually, when a nurse did come back, I was shivering so much that I couldn't control it. By then I was suffering from hypothermia, so I was wrapped completely in tin foil. It felt as if I had been prepared 'oven ready' as with a chicken. For some days the tinfoil was included in the makeup of my bed. It made a huge difference.

At some stage I was very fortunate to be given an airbed as there was a risk that I might develop bedsores, which fortunately I never did. I was also treated to the luxury of at least three pillows, even though I learned that these were in rather short supply. My treatments, I was told by Dr K, were extremely complicated as I had to be treated for the blood clots in my lungs as well as for the cancer. For the clots I needed to be given blood thinning treatment, which would reduce one of the two blood clotting systems in the body. But I then would need to recover from that before I could be given the next chemo, which would reduce the other blood clotting system. If I was depleted of both clotting systems at the same time there would be a risk of my dying from internal hemorrhage. These complications meant that the doctors had to keep a constant watch on my various blood levels, choosing the most opportune moment for each next step of the treatment: for the chemo or for dissolving the blood clots.

Margaret noticed that, for the first two months, I was too ill to know how ill I was. An example of that became apparent when I dropped something from my bed, in the night, and I didn't want to call for help. Surely, I could get out of bed to pick it up myself. But, once I was standing on my feet (the first time for quite a while) I immediately became extremely dizzy. That was the last thing I knew. I was later found, unconscious, lying on the floor. No one knew exactly how long I had been there, and I certainly didn't know.

I was frequently tested, for all manner of things, with different kinds of scan; heart echo, MRI, X-ray, C-T scan and whatever else. And my blood was tested daily. This blood was usually taken through the multiple line in my arm. But sometimes this became blocked, so the nurses had to put a cannula into a vein. Unfortunately they had to use my veins so frequently, for one thing or another, that they began to have difficulty in finding any vein that would work. I was told that this was because the chemo had the effect of shrinking my veins, making it increasingly difficult to take blood in that way. And sometimes a nurse ended up digging into my veins trying to get blood. This was the only thing that was really painful, throughout my time in hospital. Strangely, there were some nurses who were still expertly able to find blood at the first attempt, and yet others regularly had problems over this.

Several times I was found to be in need of a blood transfusion. Altogether, as I recall, I received at different times a total of 14 units. It was extraordinary knowing how many people had donated blood towards my treatment. What a gift.

For most of the first two months, looking back I now realize that I had been mostly in a kind of hibernation. I was sort of suspended this side of sleep but only fully awake and alert when I had visitors. One of the many things Margaret was doing for me, throughout, was to handle the frequent requests from people wishing to visit me. It was a huge help knowing that I would be visited but also knowing that I was being protected from too many visits on any one day. I often had just one or two in a day, each person knowing that I might only manage about half an hour or so. Quite often it was so good to see these people that I would manage longer but then I would find myself slipping back into being drowsy or falling asleep while they were there. Amazingly, Margaret never missed a single day during the time I was in hospital, in coming to visit me.

Some days I was caught into such a deep lethargy that it felt as if there might not be sufficient energy available to sustain life. On one such occasion the sense of being drained of all energy was so complete that I could not dare to sleep until I had made sure that Margaret would be able to find my wedding ring, which had to be removed. I had lost so much weight it was falling off. Only then could I give in to sleep, feeling that I might not wake.

There were several periods of time when I was faced with the real possibility that I might die. In fact, during those times when I felt able to concentrate enough to write on my iPad, I worked out details for my funeral: mainly the music. But I was in no way afraid of dying. I felt completely accepting of it. The only thing that really mattered was that I should live long enough to see our grandchildren again, and they were not due to come to England until July. In the end, I didn't leave hospital until 23rd April. But that still gave me time before they came, for me to adjust to being on my feet again and being back at home, all of which took adjusting to.

Our daughter, Bella, was in Australia with our four grandchildren. The youngest grandchild, Iona, was three when I was in hospital and she had no memory of me, so Bella brought her (along with Arthur, the eldest) so that she could have at least some memory of me, in case I died. They were in London for about ten days, which was wonderful.

For the first six or seven days, when Iona came to visit, she just stood at the end of my bed. Mostly she was staring at the strange sight of her grandfather in bed, already with very little hair, with tubes into his arm, a tube up his nose and sometimes with oxygen as well. She was silent and shy. About a week into the visit, she came to stand beside me (un-prompted by anyone) and she put both of her hands on top of mine, which was on the bedside rail. She then stood there, gazing into my eyes, unblinking and silent. It was like a healing, a laying on of hands. At the time it really felt as if she was willing me to live, and maybe she was. It was a magical moment that I have treasured ever since.

One of the things that had most preoccupied Bella when I first went into hospital was: 'Will they know who Dad is?' She kept asking this, which began to worry me. Not knowing what we could do about that, I suggested to Margaret that she bring in a copy of my last book, *Learning from life*, which could be put on my bedside table. If anyone showed interest in that, they could get some sense of me as having been someone before I became a hospital number.

Unexpectedly, that book came to be very useful to me later on. For the first two months, or more, I was so low in energy that I felt completely unable to concentrate on anything: no books, no papers, no TV and no radio or CD player. As mentioned already, I was mostly in a state of hibernation. But a time came when I began to remember Bella's concern, and I found myself thinking: 'It is not just do *they* know who I am?' but 'Do *I* know who I am?' It felt as if I had completely lost touch with my former self, feeling now reduced to this sick person in hospital, fighting to stay alive.

One day, when I was again wondering who I was, I saw the copy of my own book beside my bed. I remembered that I had loved writing it. Just maybe I might begin to get back to reading if I could read some of my own book. This may sound very self-preoccupied but it did the trick. It helped to get me back in touch with having a self, and who I used to be before my cancer.

We were not yet out of the woods with my treatment. I used to be visited most days by the physiotherapists, trying to help me recover strength in my arms and legs. Some days, when I woke early, I would lie in bed doing such exercises as I could manage. But there were some days when I had to ask them to leave my exercises for another day. I just didn't have the energy to exercise anything.

One day I woke early to find that my left arm was causing me great pain. The strange thing was that this arm was in spasm, sticking straight up, but I could not release it, to bring it down. Nor could I move anything. I found that I was completely paralyzed, unable to move anything except for my eyes; and I could not make a sound. I lay like this for about two hours until a nurse came in with my morning pills. 'Sit up,' she said, 'it's time for your pills.' I could not make any response. After repeating her command several times, and not noticing that I was in crisis, the nurse proceeded to push all the pills into my mouth and then pushed a bottle in to make me swallow them. Fortunately, I still had a swallowing reflex.

Although I experienced this pushing of pills into me as a terrible assault, it was strangely helpful in one particular way. I was so angry about this, I struggled to protest, and that struggle somehow began to join me up again. After beginning to be able to make a few groaning sounds I found that my nerve connections slowly spread to my head and then to my arm. At last I could lower it and begin to get the blood back into my hand. The pain began to subside.

No one seemed to understand what had happened and neither did I. And this same paralysis happened again a few days later, again for about two hours, but I was then not so alarmed as I knew I had come out of it before. But the first time was an extraordinary opportunity to experience, first hand, the terrors that locked-in patients must go through. I subsequently begged the doctors to note that if I ever got stuck in that state irreparably I wished to have DNR (do not resuscitate) recorded on my notes.

One day, when the physiotherapists were again trying to help me to recover use of my legs, I was standing at a Zimmer while trying to walk on the spot. I then found that I began to feel dizzy; very dizzy; very, very dizzy. I told the physio of this, as it increased, and then I remembered no more.

I learned later that the physio got me seated and then found that I had stopped breathing, and 'showed no vital signs'. It seems that I had gone into 'arrest'. She immediately called the crash team which, I was told, were there within two minutes. Meanwhile, Margaret was telephoned and it was suggested she came to the hospital as soon as possible. When she arrived, she found the crash team still working on me. I don't know what they did, but they got me back. I later learned that the physiotherapist who had been with me had undoubtedly saved my life by acting so promptly.

I continued to have problems in recovering the use of my legs. This had presented a regular problem when it came to weighing me. The nurses didn't always have time to find the weighing chair, so they made do by holding me onto floor scales, while I bounced up and down unable to stand properly, and they would note the swings on the scales, estimating my weight as being mid-way between the extremes.

We then came to the moment of decision about whether to continue with the chemo treatment or to discontinue it. Until then I had been accepting that a lot of people learn to live with cancer, so I surely could do the same. I therefore told my consultant (Dr K) I was prepared for the possibility that I might have to return, from time to time, for more chemo. Why should I expect it to be any different from how it is for most cancer people? However Dr K was very direct with me, as always. She explained that, with my cancer, there is only one chance to 'get' it. Either we eliminate the cancer or the cancer would eliminate me. She also explained that I should not think of coming back for more chemo treatments in future. As I understood it, she would not be able to give me any more chemo treatment after the course I was on. I think this may have been because of the risks to my heart. So, when we were coming up to the point of my having the last of the four chemos in my treatment, Dr K came to see me along with Margaret to explain the options. From the last scan it was evident that my cancer was still active. So the choice was as follows: either we let the cancer have its way, which should give us some weeks or months to prepare for my dying. Or, if we went for the final chemo, I might be dead in a matter of days. 'So, don't be greedy for life,' she said. She had presented the clinical picture to a group of consultants and they were apparently completely split between a definite 'don't go there' and 'give it a try'.

Margaret and I thought carefully about the options and decided to let the family know we were going for the slow route to death, with the advantage of having time to prepare for it.

However, the following day, Dr K came to let us know that the latest echo test on my heart had come back with a slightly more encouraging reading. This might give us a chance of risking the fourth chemo. We therefore decided to go for it, and we had to go through the process of letting the family know we were no longer preparing for my possible death in a few months. But, I might still be dead in a few days. We went for it and I didn't die.

There came a time, towards the end of my five months in hospital, when I was beginning to make progress on the Zimmer. Having needed two people to hold me, at first, I had got to the stage where one was enough. Then I was told that I could have a go on my own, next day, as long as there was someone in the room with me.

A lovely Irish nurse was there when I tried my first solo attempt with the Zimmer. He watched me, no doubt seeing the eagerness in my eye as I began my first steps towards getting out of hospital, and he remarked: 'Look at you with that Zimmer. You are going along like a snail with a hard-on.' I nearly fell over I laughed so much.

Mostly I was treated extremely well. But there was one relief consultant, who was dreadful. He twice visited me without giving me a chance to speak to him. The first time was when I was cleaning my teeth. He just spoke to my back and disappeared. The second time I was sitting down and he again spoke to the back of my head. This time I protested, saying I didn't want him to say another word until I could see his face. He claimed that there was no way he could get to where I could see his face, but a registrar took charge and moved the bedside table so that he could stand in front of me.

I later complained about this to my lovely Dr K. She said I could either write a formal complaint or I could ask to speak to him. I chose to see him face to face. In the meantime, I had learned that this consultant used to have a good reputation for his bedside manner. So, when we met, I said to him that, as an analyst, I had been interested to hear he had once been particularly well thought of for his bedside manner, but I had been told that about two years ago he seemed to have lost that skill. 'I don't want to know what has happened to you, but I do think you owe it to yourself, and to your patients, to think about that change, you giving up on such an important skill.' I was pleased to find that this consultant did not retreat into being defensive. He listened to what I was saying and he assured me he would think carefully about it. I was glad we were able to part on an amicable basis.

Towards the end of my time at the Royal Free I was sent to the Marie Curie Hospice (Eden Hall) for rehabilitation, mainly to help me get to the point of being able to manage the stairs. This wasn't really as helpful as it might have been. For some reason, I didn't get any access to the gym. By this time, I was almost through my hospital time, but not quite. One day, in Eden Hall, I was (a second time) found unconscious on the floor. I had passed out once more and my pulse was again found to be 220.

This led to my being referred back to the RFH, once more in the heart unit, where I was eventually given 'cardioversion'. This was amazing. I came to after the anaesthetic and my head had become completely clear, such as it hadn't been for all the time I was in hospital. It seems that my cancer had affected my heart and my central nervous system, but at least the arrhythmia had been cleared. However, I had learned that the chemo had somewhat reduced my heart function. And I was later to find that I had also lost proper control of my legs, needing always to have a walking stick to catch me when I begin to stumble. I now regard my legs as having become *adolescent*. 'They won't always do what I tell them to do.' But all of that is but a small price to pay for life.

I was finally sent for a further CT scan, again at UCH where they have that most advanced scanner. This would tell us if my cancer was still active or, maybe, that it had been eliminated.

We had to wait for a further consultation with Dr K. The results she would be giving us could not have been more totally 'life or death', as it had been made clear to us that, if the cancer was still active, I could not be given any more chemo, then or ever.

Margaret and I went for the consultation to be told these results. Of course, we were both very anxious, so it was not surprising that we arrived an hour early for our appointment. We then saw Dr K come out to collect her next patient. But, when she saw us sitting at the back of the waiting room, she didn't turn away from us, as some doctors might have done. She came straight over with a broad smile on her face. She said she didn't want us to have to wait until the time of our appointment, so she was telling us straight away that the scan was completely clear. Wasn't that the best doctoring possible? Just imagine the hell we might have gone through if Dr K had turned her back on us, it not yet being our time to see her.

When we eventually saw Dr K she said that I had made another patient very unhappy. How was that? She then told us that she had another patient who, previously, had been the oldest person she had known to survive their most aggressive chemo. He had been seventy-two at the time. She had just been seeing him and he had told her how proud he was to have achieved that special place in medicine. 'Unfortunately,' she had to tell him, 'that place has now been taken by another.' I was then seventy-seven. Dr K also spelled out to us, something she had chosen not to tell us before, that I had initially been deemed to have 'less than a 3% chance of survival' because of the advanced state of my cancer when we first knew of it and because of the other complications that came to be involved, my heart and the clots in my lungs.

So, how good it is to be still alive.

Notes

1   First published on *Karnacology*, website of Karnac Books. Reprinted by permission of Karnac Books.
2   When Dr K gave permission for this to be first published she specifically asked that her identity should remain anonymous.

Bibliography

Alexander, F. (1954). Some quantitative aspects of psychoanalytic technique. *Journal of the American Psychoanalytical Association*, 2: 685–701.

Baker, R. (2000). Finding the neutral position. *Journal of the American Psychoanalytical Association*, 48: 129–153.

Bion, W.R. (1967). *Second thoughts*. New York: Aronson.

Boesky, D. (2006). Psychoanalytic controversies contextualized. *Journal of the American Psychoanalytic Association*, 53(3): 835–863.

Bollas, C. (1987). *The shadow of the object*. London: Free Association Books.

Casement, P.J. (1964). A false security? *Prism*, 88: 28–30.

Casement, P.J. (1969). The setting of limits: a belief in growth. *Case Conference*, 16(7): 267–271.

Casement, P.J. (1985; 1991). *On learning from the patient*. London: Tavistock Publications.

Casement, P.J. (1990). *Further learning from the patient*. London: Routledge.

Casement, P.J. (1991). *Learning from the patient*. New York: Guilford Publications.

Casement, P.J. (1993). Psychoanalysis: procedure or process? *Psyche*, 11: 1013–1026.

Casement, P.J. (2002). *Learning from our mistakes: beyond dogma in psychoanalysis and psychotherapy*. London: Routledge.

Casement, P.J. (2006). *Learning from life: becoming a psychoanalyst*. London: Routledge.

Casement, P.J. (2009). Beyond words: the role of psychoanalysis. *The Psychologist*, 22, May: 404–405.

Casement, P.J. (2009). Seeking a balance between knowing and not knowing in the consulting room. *Hellenic Journal of Psychology*, 6: 334–347.

Casement, P.J. (2011). Imprisoned minds. *American Imago*, 68(2): 287–295.

Casement, P.J. (2015). *Growing up? A journey with laughter*. London: Karnac Books

Casement, P.J. (2017). Ways of working. *International Journal of Psycho-Analysis*, 98(6): 1813–1815.

Casement, P.J. (in press). Keeping in mind. In *'Out of hours': between boundary attunement and a paradigm shift in psychoanalysis and psychotherapy*. (eds.) Sinason, V. & Sachs, A. London: Routledge.

Couch, A.S. (1995). Anna Freud's adult psychoanalytic technique: a defence of classical analysis. *International Journal of Psycho-Analysis*, 76: 153–171.

Crick, P. (1991). Good supervision: on the experience of being supervised. *Psychoanalytic Psychotherapy*, 5: 235–245.

Eisold, K. (1994). The intolerance of diversity in psychoanalytic institutes. *International Journal of Psycho-Analysis*, 75: 785–800.

Fairbairn, W.R.D. (1963) Synopsis of an object-relations theory of the personality of his theoretical position. *International Journal of Psycho-Analysis*, 44: 224–225.

Fox, R.P. (1984). The principle of abstinence reconsidered. *International Journal of Psycho-Analysis*, 11: 227-236.

Franklin, G. (1990). The multiple meanings of neutrality. *Journal of the American Psycho-analytic Association*, 38: 195-220.

Garza-Guerrero, C. (2002). The crisis in psychoanalysis: what crisis are we talking about? *International Journal of Psycho-Analysis*, 83: 57–83.

Garza-Guerrero, C. (2004). Reorganizational and educational demands of psychoanalytic training today: our long and marasmic night of one century. *International Journal of Psycho-Analysis*, 85: 3–13.

Heimann, P. (1950). On counter-transference. *International Journal of Psycho-Analysis*, 31: 81–84.

Hewison, D. (2003). Book review of *Learning from our mistakes: beyond dogma in psychoanalysis and psychotherapy* (Casement, 2002). *Journal of Analytical Psychology*, 48(5): 729–730.

Hymer, Sharon M. (2004). The imprisoned self. *Psychoanalytic Review*, 91: 683–697.

Kernberg, O. (1986). Institutional problems of psychoanalytic education. *Journal of the American Psychoanalytic Association*, 34: 799–834.

Kernberg, O. (1996a). Thirty methods to destroy the creativity of psychoanalytic students. *International Journal of Psycho-Analysis*, 77: 1031–1040.

Kernberg, O. (1996b). The analyst's authority in the psychoanalytic situation. *Psycho-analytic Quarterly*, 65: 137–157.

Kernberg, O. (2000). A concerned critique of psychoanalytic education. *International Journal of Psycho-Analysis*, 81: 97–120.

Kernberg, O. (2001). Some thoughts regarding innovations in psychoanalytic education. Presentation at the IPA Executive Council meeting, in Puerto Vallarta, 7 January.

Khan, M.M.R. (1963). The concept of cumulative trauma. *Psychoanalytic Study of the Child*, 18: 286–306.

Khan, M.M.R. (1973). *The privacy of the self*. London: Hogarth Press.

King, P. (1978). Affective response of the analyst to the patient's communications. *International Journal of Psycho-Analysis*, 59: 329–334.

King, P. (1989). On being a psychoanalyst: integrity and vulnerability in psychoanalytic organizations. In *The psychoanalytic core: essays in honour of Leo Rangell, MD.* (eds.) Harold P. Blum, Edward M. Weinshel & F. Robert Rodman. London: International Universities Press: 331-51

King, P. (1991). Conclusions. In *The Freud-Klein controversies 1941–45.* (eds.) P. King & R. Steiner. London/New York: Routledge: 920–931.

Kirsner, D. (2000). *Unfree associations*. London: Process Press.

Klein, M. (1946). Notes on some schizoid mechanisms. *International Journal of Psycho-Analysis*, 27: 99–110.

Kohon, G. (ed.) (1986). *The British school of psycho-analysis: the independent tradition.* London: Free Association Books.

Langs, R.J. (1978). *The listening process*. New York: Aronson.

Little, M. (1951). Counter-transference and the patient's response to it. *International Journal of Psycho-Analysis*, 32: 32–40.

Pizer, S.A. (2004). Learning from our mistakes: beyond dogma in psychoanalysis and psychotherapy (review). *American Imago*, 61(4): 543–556.

Popper, K.R. (1974 [1957]). *The poverty of historicism*. London: Routledge and Kegan Paul.

Racker, H. (1957). The meanings and uses of counter-transference. *Psychoanalytic Quarterly*, 26: 303–357.

Racker, H. (1968). *Transference and counter-transference*. London: Hogarth Press.

Rayner, E. (1992). Matching, attunement and the psychoanalytic dialogue. *International Journal of Psycho-Analysis*, 73: 39–54.

Sandler, J. (1976). Counter-transference and role-responsiveness. *International Journal of Psycho-Analysis*, 3: 43–47.

Shmukler, D. (2016). *Supervision in psychoanalysis and psychotherapy: a case study and clinical guide*. London: Routledge.

Sterba, R. (1934). The fate of the ego in analytic therapy. *International Journal of Psycho-Analysis*, 15: 117–126.

Stewart, H. (1992). *Psychic experience and problems of technique*. London: Routledge.

Symington, N. (1986). *The analytic experience*. London: Free Association Books.

Target, M. (2001). Some issues in psychoanalytic training: an overview of the literature and some resulting observations. 2nd Joseph Sandler Research Conference, UCL 10th March.

Thompson, C. (1958). A study of the emotional climate of psychoanalytic institutes. *Psychiatry*, 21: 45–51.

Tipple, R. (2017). Art therapy. *Art Therapy On Line* (ATOL), 8(1).

Tuckett, D. (2005). Does anything go? Towards a framework for the more transparent assessment of psychoanalytic competence. *International Journal of Psycho-Analysis*, 86: 31–49.

Widlöcher, D. (1978). The ego ideal of the psychoanalyst. *International Journal of Psycho-Analysis*, 59: 387–390.

Winnicott, D.W. (1948). Hate in the counter-transference. In Winnicott (1958): 194–203.

Winnicott, D.W. (1955). Metapsychological and clinical aspects of regression within the analytical set-up. *International Journal of Psycho-Analysis*, 36: 16–26.

Winnicott, D.W. (1958). *Collected papers: through paediatrics to psycho-analysis*. London: Tavistock Publications.

Winnicott, D.W. (1965). *Maturational processes and the facilitating environment*. London: Tavistock Publications.

Winnicott, D.W. (1971 [1969]). The use of an object and relating through identifications. In *Playing and reality*. London: Tavistock: 86–94.

Winnicott, D.W. (1971). *Playing and reality*. London: Tavistock.

Winnicott, D. W. (1974). Fear of breakdown. *International Review of Psychoanalysis*, 1: 103–107.

Index

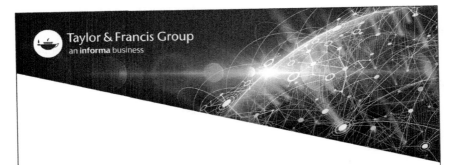